A bright lantern shining in the dark night,
offering warm hospitality
and sustenance to our guests . . .

A Gift from
Rabbit Hill
-1990

I_n T_{ribute} . . .

Norman T. Simpson was and remains an inspiration to innkeepers
and inngoers everywhere. Credited
with having sparked the renaissance
of the American village inn with his
book, Country Inns and Back
Roads, *he has pointed the way for a
generation of travelers and innkeepers who want a friendlier, more
personal kind of hospitality.*

*In 1966 when he held a dinner
for the tiny group of innkeepers who
were included in the 16-page booklet
that was the first edition of* Country
Inns and Back Roads, *little did he
or they realize that it was the first
meeting of what was to become offi-
cially in 1972 the Independent Innkeepers' Association. As the book ex-*

*panded with more and more country inns, so the innkeepers' gatherings
grew and became more structured.*

*In those early years, and subsequently, it was clear that the 3-day
annual and numerous regional meetings led by Norman were important
sources of renewal and support, and much needed by the innkeepers.
Certain principles and values emerged over the years as important in
Norman's selection of inns. First and foremost, among many others, are
the innkeepers, whose inns are reflections of themselves in all aspects of
innkeeping.*

*It is in the hands of those innkeepers, members of the Independent
Innkeepers' Association, that Norman Simpson left his legacy. The IIA is
pledged to uphold the principles and goals of innkeeping that he advo-
cated, and to carry forward the tradition of warm, personal hospitality
that was so treasured by this genial, gentle man, rightfully called "the
father of country inns."*

The Innkeepers' Register

1989-90

Country Inns of North America

Independent Innkeepers' Association
Stockbridge, Massachusetts
Founded in 1972
by
Norman T. Simpson

COVER DESIGN: Helene Verin

ILLUSTRATIONS: Janice Lindstrom

EDITORS: Virginia Rowe, Allan Smith

THE INNKEEPERS' REGISTER—COUNTRY INNS OF NORTH AMERICA, 1989-90
Copyright © 1989 by the Independent Innkeepers' Association. All rights reserved.
Published by Berkshire Traveller Press, Stockbridge, Massachusetts 01262. Printed in
the United States of America by The Studley Press, Dalton, Massachusetts

ISBN 0-930145-00-3
Library of Congress No. 89-61363

For further information, call Independent Innkeepers' Association, 800-344-5244

CONTENTS

UNITED STATES

CANADA

We regret we were unable to include the following inns who are also members of the IIA in good standing.

GREY ROCK INN
Janet Millett
Harborside Road
Northeast Harbor, ME 04662
207-276-9360

INN AT LITTLE WASHINGTON
Reinhardt Lynch/Patrick O'Connell
Box 300
Middle Street
Washington, VA 22747
703-675-3800

L'AUBERGE DU ROY
Jean-Claud & Isabele Lisita
106 Rue St. Laurent
Deschambault, Canada G0A 1S0
418-286-6958

OBAN INN
Gary Burroughs
Niagara-on-the-Lake, Ontario
Canada L0S 1J0
416-468-2165

THE OPINICON
Al & Janice Cross
Chaffey's Locks, RR1
Elgin, Canada K0G 1C0
613-359-5233

KEY TO SYMBOLS

	ENGLISH	FRENCH	GERMAN	JAPANESE	SPANISH
	number of rooms; rates and rate plan for 2 people number of suites; rates and rate plan for 2 people credit cards accepted	nombre de chambres, les prix pour deux personnes, plan de repas; nombre d'appartements, les prix pour deux personnes, plan de repas les cartes de crédit acceptées	Anzahl des Zimmers; Tarif-und Tarifplan Anzahl der Zimmerflüchte; Tarif-und Tarifplan Kreditkarten angenommen	部屋数：宿泊料金と料金別プラン スイート数：宿泊金と料金別プラン クレジットカード通用	número de habitaciones; tarifas y tablas de tarifas para dos personas número de apartamentos; tarifas y tablas de tarifas para dos personas tarjetas de crédito que aceptamos
	baths—private/shared	salle de bains et WC privés ou communs	Bäder privat/geteilt	バス付 / 共同バス	habitaciones con baño / sin baño
	open/close	période de fermeture ou ouverture	offen: geschlossen	営業中/休業ー シーズン	temporado—fecha en que se abre / fecha en que se cierra
	children and pets acceptability, inquire for rates	les enfants admis? chiens admis? renseignez-vous sur les tarrifs	Kinder und Haustiere erlaubt; nach Tarifen erkundigen	子供とペット可、別料金	reglamentos para niños y animales domésticos (pídase tarifas)
	recreation and attractions on premises or in area	les sports et les divertissements à l'hôtel ou l'environs	Erhohlung und Schenswürdigkeiten; an Ort und Stelle oder im Gegend	当地のレクレーション・催し物	atracciones y diversions / en los terrenos o cercanos
	meals available; wine & liquor available	repas offerts et bar sur place	Speise und Spirituosen erhältlich	食事と飲食可	comida y licores en venta / no se venden
	smoking acceptability	fumer permis?	Rauchen erlaubt/ begrenzt/verboten	喫煙可	se puede fumar / no se puede fumar
	special features, i.e., wheelchair access; conference facilities	installation, accès de l'handicapés physiques, les séminaires reçus, capacité	Sondermerkungen; Rollstuhl Zugang, z.B. Konferenzräume	特別施設 会議室 車イス出入口	a notar: acceso para sillas de ruedas, facilidades para conferencias
MAP	Modified American Plan	breakfast & dinner included in rate demi-pension Frühstück und Abendessen im Preis inbegriffen 特別アメリカプランー朝・夕食付 la tarifa incluye cena y desayuno			
AP	American Plan	3 meals included in rate pension complète (3) drei Mahlzeiten im Preis inbegriffen アメリカプランー3食付 la tarifa comprende desayuno, almuerzo y cena			
EP	European Plan	no meals included in rate les repas ne sont pas compris Keine Mahlzeiten im Preis inbegriffen ヨーロッパプランー食事なし la tarifa no incluye comida alguna			
B&B	Bed & Breakfast	breakfast included in rate le petit déjeuner est compris inbegriffen 朝食付 la tarifa incluye el desayuno			

RESERVATION AND RATE INFORMATION

Rates listed herein represent a general range of rates for two people for one night at each inn, and should not be considered firm quotations. The rates cover both high and low seasons; tax and gratuities are usually not included. It is well to inquire as to the availability of various special plans and packages. Please be aware that reservation and cancellation policies vary from inn to inn. Listed recreation and attractions are either on the premises or nearby. For more detailed information, ask for inn brochure.

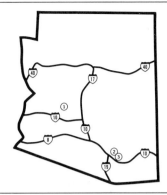

The Lodge on the Desert

The feeling of Old Mexico and of the Southwest is everywhere in the adobe-colored casas grouped around intimate patios at this Mexican-hacienda-style resort-inn. Magnificent mountain and desert views, spacious lawns, and colorful gardens belie the proximity of fine residences and nearby downtown Tucson, with all its cultural and recreational attractions.

 33 rooms, $46/$119 B&B
7 suites, $60/$125 B&B
Visa, MC, Amex, Diners, CB

 all private baths

 open year-round

children welcome
pets by prior arrangement

 heated swimming pool, croquet
golf, tennis, racquet ball
shuffleboard, ping-pong

 breakfast, lunch, dinner
AP & MAP available 11/1—5/15
wine & liquor available

smoking accepted

wheelchair access (7 rooms)
conference facilities (40)

From I-10 take Speedway. exit,
5 mi. (E) to R. turn (S) at Alvernon
Wy. Continue .8 mi. to Lodge on L.
between 5th St. and Broadway.

603-325-3366 or 800-456-5634
306 N. Alvernon Way, P.O. Box 42500, Tucson, AZ 85733
Schuyler & Helen Lininger, Innkeepers

Rancho de los Caballeros

A green jewel in the desert, with an 18-hole championship golf course, tennis courts, trail rides and other planned activities for adults and children, this rambling ranch-resort has been run by the same family since its inception in 1948. Individual bungalows and terraces, poolside buffet lunches, and evening cookouts brighten winter vacations.

 74 rooms, $90/$160 AP
12 suites, $150/$230 AP
no credit cards

 all private baths

 closed mid-May to Oct. 1

 children welcome
no pets

 18-hole golf, riding, 4 tennis
courts, heated pool, skeet &
trap shooting

 all meals AP
wine & liquor available

 smoking accepted

wheelchair access
conference facilities (275)

In Wickenburg, take U.S. 60 2 mi.
(W) of light, turn L. (S) on Vulture
Mine Rd. Continue 2 mi. to ranch
sign & entrance.

602-684-5484
P.O. Box 1148, Wickenburg, AZ 85358
Dallas C. Gant, Jr., Innkeeper

Tanque Verde Ranch

In a wild setting of desert and mountains, this 100-year-old ranch evokes the spirit of the Old West. Horseback riding, guided nature hikes, bird study programs, as well as a modern health spa, tennis, in- and outdoor pools, great food, and a casual, relaxed atmosphere mean good times for lucky guests. It's been given a 4-star rating by Mobil.

 44 rooms, $139/$209 AP
16 suites, $159/$249 AP
Visa, MC, Amex

 all private baths

 open year-round

 children & families welcome
no pets

 riding (115 horses), 5 tennis
courts, health spa, pool

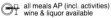 all meals AP (incl. activities)
wine & liquor available

smoking accepted

 wheelchair access (56 rooms)
conference facilities (120)

In Tucson, take Speedway. Blvd. (E)
to dead end at ranch.

602-296-6275
14301 E. Speedway Blvd., Tucson, AZ 85748
Robert Cote, Innkeeper

CALIFORNIA

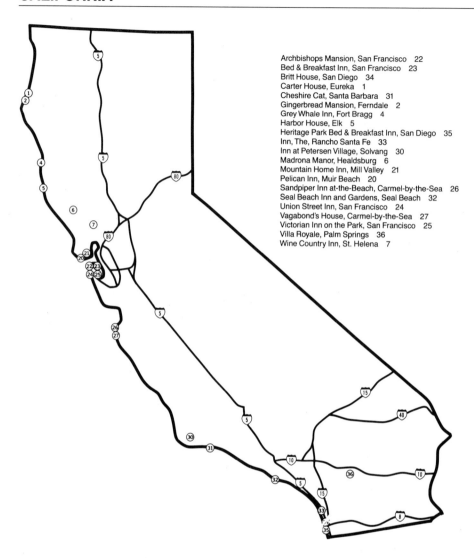

Archbishops Mansion, San Francisco   22
Bed & Breakfast Inn, San Francisco   23
Britt House, San Diego   34
Carter House, Eureka   1
Cheshire Cat, Santa Barbara   31
Gingerbread Mansion, Ferndale   2
Grey Whale Inn, Fort Bragg   4
Harbor House, Elk   5
Heritage Park Bed & Breakfast Inn, San Diego   35
Inn, The, Rancho Santa Fe   33
Inn at Petersen Village, Solvang   30
Madrona Manor, Healdsburg   6
Mountain Home Inn, Mill Valley   21
Pelican Inn, Muir Beach   20
Sandpiper Inn at-the-Beach, Carmel-by-the-Sea   26
Seal Beach Inn and Gardens, Seal Beach   32
Union Street Inn, San Francisco   24
Vagabond's House, Carmel-by-the-Sea   27
Victorian Inn on the Park, San Francisco   25
Villa Royale, Palm Springs   36
Wine Country Inn, St. Helena   7

Archbishops Mansion

Surrounded by an operatic opulence that delights the senses, the guest in this splendid mansion, which was indeed the home of archbishops, is pampered in every way. Guest rooms are exquisite, with the most luxurious accouterments. The welcome is gracious and informal, making everyone feel at ease.

 10 rooms, $100/$159 B&B
5 suites, $189/$285 B&B
Visa, MC, Amex

 expanded continental breakfast
wine available

all private baths, 3 Jacuzzis

open year-round

 conference facilities (30)
private parking

children accepted
no pets

From airport, take Hwy. 101 to Fell St. exit, 5 blocks R. (N) on Steiner, 2 blocks L. (W) on Fulton.

 shopping, theater, museums

415-563-7872; for reservations: 800-543-5820
1000 Fulton St., San Francisco, CA 94117
Jonathan Shannon & Jeffrey Ross, Innkeepers

The Bed and Breakfast Inn

Tucked into a quiet "mews" right in the middle of a trendy San Francisco shopping area, these 3 pre-earthquake Victorians were the only bed and breakfast in the city for many years. Cozy, bright rooms and the cheerful, friendly staff, along with innkeepers Bob and Marily Kavanaugh, make a trip to the big city easy and fun.

 5 rooms, $72/$108 B&B
5 suites, $124/$184 B&B
no credit cards

 6 private, 3 shared baths

 open year-round

 children over 11
no pets

San Francisco & all its attractions

 breakfast
sherry in rooms

smoking accepted

wheelchair access (2 rooms)

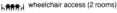 In S.F. follow all "Golden Gate Bridge" signs. Turn at Franklin & continue to Union St. L. to Laguna. Inn is between Laguna & Buchanan.

415-921-9784
4 Charlton Court, San Francisco, CA 94123
Robert & Marily Kavanaugh, Innkeepers

Britt House

A fine example of a Queen Anne Victorian, surrounded by formal English gardens, this B&B has antiques, flowers, stuffed animals, thoughtful and humorous touches, loving pets, and a happy, energetic staff. Guests enjoy individually decorated rooms and the full breakfast and high tea. It is only 2 blocks from Balboa Park, with its world-famous zoo and Old Globe theater.

 10 rooms, $90/$110 B&B
Visa, MC, Amex

 1 private, 4 shared baths

 open year-round

children accepted
no pets

zoo, beaches, Old Globe theater, Mexico, desert

 breakfast & high tea

no smoking

 conference facilities (20)
wheelchair access (4 rooms)

Hwy. 5, Washington St. exit (from north turn l.; from south, turn R.). Head (E) on Washington St., approx. 1.5 mi. to R. (S) on 4th Ave. for approx. 1.5 mi. to NE corner 4th & Maple.

619-234-2926
406 Maple St., San Diego, CA 92103
Daun Martin, Innkeeper

Carter House

A remarkable and exact replica of an 1884 San Francisco mansion, Carter House sits on a gentle hillside overlooking Humboldt Bay and famous Carson Mansion. Exquisite antiques and delightful food have won much praise. The Carter Hotel next door, another marvelous replica, offers more rooms with telephones, TV, and conference facilities.

 6 rooms, $68/$135 B&B
1 suite, $140/$165 B&B
Visa, MC, Amex

 private & shared baths; 1 Jacuzzi

 open year-round

 children over 10
no pets

redwood forests, isolated beaches, unique shopping, galleries

 breakfast & dinner
wine & cordials available

smoking in restricted areas

 wheelchair access (2 rooms)
conference facilities (20)

 From Hwy. 101 (N) (5th St.) turn L. on "L" St. From Hwy. 101 (S) (4th St.) turn R. on "L" St. Inn is at 3rd & "L" Sts.

707-445-1390
1033 Third St., Eureka, CA 95501
Mark & Christi Carter, Innkeepers

Cheshire Cat Inn

In the lovely old Spanish town of Santa Barbara on the California coast, two Victorian houses on a quiet residential street provide charming and elegant quarters for the discerning traveler. Laura Ashley fabrics and papers, English antiques, fireplaces, patios, gardens, and an outside spa are just a few of the delights at this romantic bed and breakfast inn.

 7 rooms, $89/$169 B&B
4 suites, $129/$179 B&B
no credit cards

all private baths; 2 Jacuzzis

closed Thanksgiving, Christmas Eve & Day

no children
no pets

outside spa, croquet, bicycles, tennis, golf, boating, fishing

 breakfast
complimentary wine on Sat.
complimentary liquors

smoking on patio only

 conference facilities (22)

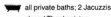 Hwy. 101 (N) exit Arrellaga (E) .4 mi. to Chapala .1 mi. to Valerio. Hwy. 101 (S) exit Mission (E) .3 mi. to De La Vina .3 mi. (S) to Valerio.

805-569-1610
36 W. Valerio St., Santa Barbara, CA 93101
Chris Dunstan, Owner; George Mari, Innkeeper

The Gingerbread Mansion

From its wonderfully intricate gingerbread architecture to its spectacular bathrooms to its 30-foot-high fuchsias in formal English gardens, this most-photographed Victorian inn is a showplace in a historic Victorian village. The feeling is comfortable, warm, and light, with turn-down service, "his & her" bubble baths by the fire, bicycles, and even rubber boots & umbrellas for rainy days.

 5 rooms, $75/$110 B&B
4 suites, $115/$150 B&B
Visa, MC, Amex

 all private baths

 open year-round

 children over 9
no pets

 games, library, bicycles, English garden, redwood parks, beach, fishing

breakfast, afternoon tea & cake

no smoking

Hwy. 101, 15 mi. south of Eureka, take Ferndale exit. Continue over bridge 5 mi. to Main St. Turn L at blue Bank of America. Go 1 block.

707-786-4000
400 Berding St., Ferndale, CA 95536-0040
Wendy Hatfield & Ken Torbert, Innkeepers

Grey Whale Inn

The Mendocino coast, with its dining, shopping, Skunk Train through the redwood forest, secluded ocean beaches, whale-watching, and state parks, is an ideal vacation spot. In this 4-story, 1915 redwood inn guests will find different features in every room: fireplace, sundeck, whirlpool tub, a garden, or ocean views. The buffet breakfast includes scrumptious, prizewinning sweet breads.

 14 rooms, $60/$125 B&B
Visa, MC, Amex

 all private baths; 1 Jacuzzi

open year-round

children over 12
no pets

 TV theater with VCR, recreation room with pool table, fishing, hiking, whale-watching

buffet breakfast
complimentary wines for special occasions

no smoking

 wheelchair access (1 room)
conference facilities (34)

Hwy. 101 to Cloverdale, then Hwy. 128 (W) to Hwy. 1. Continue (N) to Fort Bragg (3½ hrs. from S.F.). Or Hwy. 1 along the coast (5 hrs. from S.F.).

707-964-0640 (CA: 800-382-7244)
615 No. Main St., Fort Bragg, CA 95437
John & Colette Bailey, Innkeepers

Harbor House Inn by the Sea

Dramatic ocean views, where massive rocks jut from the sea, benches along a winding wildflower-edged path down to a private beach, quiet moments for solitude and reflection—all of this and more at this gracious inn, built entirely of virgin redwood. Add a quality of old-fashioned comfort with fireplaces and superbly fresh cuisine for just a hint of the pleasures that await you.

10 rooms, $115/$200 MAP
no credit cards

all private baths

open year-round

children over 15
no pets

private beach, kayaking, wineries, galleries, golf, riding

breakfast & dinner
wine & beer available

no smoking in dining room

From S.F., 3 hrs. (N) on Hwy. 101. In Cloverdale take Hwy. 128 (W) to Hwy. 1 (S) 5 mi. to Elk.

707-877-3203
Box 369, 5600 S. Highway One, Elk, CA 95432
Dean & Helen Turner, Innkeepers

Heritage Park Bed & Breakfast Inn

In a 7-acre park formed for the preservation of endangered Victorian mansions, this splendidly restored B&B offers a quiet escape in the middle of Old Town San Diego. Special occasion packages and authentic period antiques beguile guests, along with the prizewinning Strawberry Jam Loaf at breakfast and a romantic 5-course candlelight dinner or a scrumptious Victorian country supper.

 9 rooms, $75/$115 B&B
Visa, MC

 private & shared baths

 open year-round

 children over 11
no pets

 golf, beaches, tennis whale-watching, biking

 breakfast & dinner

 no smoking

 conference facilities (18)

I-5(S) to Old Town Ave exit; L. (E) to San Diego Ave. & L. again for 1 mi. to Harney St. & turn R. into park.

619-295-7088
2470 Heritage Park Row, San Diego, CA 92110
Lori Chandler, Innkeeper

The Inn at Rancho Santa Fe

Sunshine, flowers, towering eucalyptus, citrus groves—California at its best—is the story here. On 20 acres of manicured lawns and gardens, individually decorated guest cottages with secluded porches and patios are close to pool, tennis, croquet, and the elegant living room, dining room, and library. The mood is tranquil, but with many diversions.

 75 rooms, $90/$165 EP
8 suites, $235 & up EP
Visa, MC, Amex

 all private baths

 open year-round

 children accepted

tennis, swimming, golf, beaches, shopping

 breakfast, lunch, dinner
wine & liquor available

 smoking accepted

 conference facilities (100)

San Diego Freewy. (I-5) to Lomas Santa Fe Dr. Continue 6 mi. (E) inland to Rancho Santa Fe and the inn. Street name changes to Linea del Cielo in Rancho Santa Fe.

619-756-1131; FAX: 619-759-1604
5951 Linea del Cielo, Box 869, Rancho Santa Fe, CA 92067
Daniel Royce, Innkeeper

The Inn at Petersen Village

This European-style hotel overlooks an enclave of shops, arcades, and a courtyard that makes up Petersen Village, set in the heart of a Danish community in central California. On the 2nd and 3rd floors, tastefully decorated inner guest rooms circling the courtyard have views of trees, flowers, and the fountain, while those on the outer side look toward the Santa Inez mountains.

 42 rooms, $85/$140 B&B
1 suite, $185 B&B
Visa, MC, Amex

 all private baths, 1 Jacuzzi

 open year-round

 children over 6
no pets

outdoor summer theater, wineries, shops & galleries, restaurants horse-drawn trolley tours, bicycling, glider & balloon rides

 breakfast, cheese & wine
wine available

 smoking allowed

conference facilities

From Hwy. 101 take Rte. 246 for 2 mi. to Solvang.

805-688-3121 (in Calif: 800-321-8985)
1576 Mission Drive, Solvang, CA 93463
The Petersen Family, Innkeepers

Madrona Manor

This majestic Victorian manor, listed on the National Register of Historic Places, conveys a sense of homey elegance and gracious hospitality, thick terry robes, expansive breakfasts, unique and tantalizing cuisine, and beautiful views of the mountains and surrounding Sonoma wine country.

 20 rooms, $90/$136 B&B
2 suites, $95/$141 B&B
Visa, MC, Amex, Diners

 all private baths

open year-round

 children accepted
leashed dogs, outer bldgs.

swimming pool, billiards, tennis, golf, antiquing, wine tasting, canoeing

 breakfast for guests only;
dinner & Sun. brunch
wine & beer available

 smoking in restricted areas

 wheelchair access (1 room)
full conference facilities (40)

Rte. 101 (N) to Central Healdsburg exit. At 3-way light, sharp L. on Mill St., ¾ mi. to arch.

707-433-4231
1001 Westside Rd., Healdsburg, CA 95448
John & Carol Muir, Innkeepers

Mountain Home Inn

The stunning panoramic view of San Francisco Bay from this aerie on Mt. Tamalpais is breathtaking. Adjacent to a wonderful mountain and giant redwood wilderness, this multilevel, modern-rustic inn, built around 4 huge redwood trees, has many rooms with balconies and some with whirlpools or oak-burning fireplaces. Fresh fish is one of the specialties of the French/California cuisine.

 10 rooms, $108/$178 B&B
Visa, MC

 all private baths

 open year-round

 children over 12
no pets

hiking, biking, beaches, wineries, riding, San Francisco

 complimentary breakfast
lunch & dinner

no smoking in dining areas

 wheelchair access (1 room)
conference facilities (40)

From Golden Gate Bridge, 4.1 mi. (N) Hwy. 1 exit. L. at light for 2.6 mi. Turn R. onto Panoramic for .8 mi. At junction take high road.

415-381-9000
810 Panoramic Hwy., Mill Valley, CA 94941
Susan & Ed Cunningham, Innkeepers

Pelican Inn

A scant 10 mi. from Golden Gate Bridge, in the sea-blown fog of Muir Beach, among pine, alder, honeysuckle, and jasmine, is half-timbered Pelican Inn, reminiscent of 16th-century Tudor England. A refuge between the ocean and the great redwoods, the inn's Inglenook fireplace, country cooking, and English antiques beckon guests to carefree feasting and relaxation.

 7 rooms, $110/$135 B&B
Visa, MC

 all private baths

 closed Christmas Day

 children welcome
no pets

 beachcombing, hiking, whale-watching

complimentary breakfast
lunch & dinner
wine & beer available

 conference facilities (40)

In S.F. 4.1 mi. north of Golden Gate Bridge, take Hwy. 1 exit. L. at light & continue 5 mi. to inn.

415-383-6000
Muir Beach, CA 94965
Barry & Pamela Stock, Innkeepers

Sandpiper Inn at-the-Beach

Only 60 yards from Carmel's wide, white beach, with sweeping views across the bay to Pebble Beach, this European-style inn is in a beautiful, quiet residential area, near the 1770 Carmel Mission. French antiques, a library, a lounge, a garden patio, and individually decorated guest rooms and cottages, some with wood-burning fireplaces, offer a pleasant stay in a charming seaside village.

 12 rooms, $90/$140 B&B
3 suites, $140 B&B
Visa, MC, Amex

 all private baths

 open year-round

 children over 12
no pets

 Pebble Beach, golf, tennis, state parks, aquarium, walking paths

breakfast
complimentary sherry
BYOB

conference facilities (60)

Hwy. 1, R. at Ocean Ave. (W) thru Carmel 1 mi. L. at Scenic Rd. (S) .8 mi. to end of beach at Martin Way (S).

408-624-6433
2408 Bay View Ave., Carmel-by-the-Sea, CA 93923
Graeme & Irene Mackenzie, Innkeepers

The Seal Beach Inn and Gardens

The glowing colors of massed flowers and lush plantings transform the brick courtyard of this Mediterranean-style inn into a veritable fairyland, with old ornate streetlights, blue canopies, fountains, and objets d'art. A lighted kiosk posts notices of the many Southern California attractions close by. The service is thoughtful and friendly, and the breakfasts are lavish.

 11 rooms, $88/$155 B&B
11 suites, $88/$155 B&B
Visa, MC, Amex, Diners, JCB

 all private baths

 open year-round

 children over 5
pets not accepted

 pool, tennis, boating, golf, swimming, bicycles

buffet breakfast
catered meals, advance reservation

 no smoking inside

conference facilities (44)

Hwy. 405 Fwy., Seal Beach Blvd. exit, turn L. for 2.7 mi. R. on Pacific Coast Hwy. for .7 mi. L. on 5th St.

213-493-2416
212 5th St., Seal Beach, CA 90740
Marjorie & Jack Bettenhausen, Innkeepers

Union Street Inn

Combining the charm and elegance of a 19th-century Edwardian home with the friendly, personal attention of a fine European-style pension, this inn features a tranquil garden in the heart of San Francisco in historic Cow Hollow. The continental breakfast includes fresh-roasted coffee, hot breads, and fresh fruit served in the parlor, the garden, or your room.

 5 rooms, $125/$149 B&B
carriage house, $195/$225 B&B
Visa, MC, Amex

 all private baths, 2 Jacuzzis

 open year-round

 children accepted
no pets

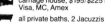 fine shopping, dining, all S.F. attractions

breakfast
wine available

 no smoking

From Hwy. 101, take Van Ness exit to Union St. Turn L. for 7 blocks. Between Fillmore & Steiner on L.

415-346-0424
2229 Union St., San Francisco, CA 94123
Helen Stewart, Innkeeper

Vagabond's House Inn

The stone courtyard here is an almost magical experience, with the great oak, surrounded by vines, ferns, and gorgeous flowers. The pet squirrel scampers by, and Tuffy, the watch cat, suns on a doorstep. Around the courtyard are unique rooms with fireplaces. All the natural beauty and fascinating shops of Carmel are just around the corner.

 11 rooms, $79/$135 B&B
Visa, MC, Amex

all private baths

open year-round

 children over 11
pets accepted

Carmel beach, 17-Mile Drive, golf, tennis, Big Sur, Monterey Bay Aquarium

 breakfast
cream sherry

smoking restricted

Turn off Hwy. 1 to Ocean Ave., (W) to town center. R. onto Dolores for 2.5 blocks to inn.

408-624-7738
P.O. Box 2747, Dolores & 4th, Carmel, CA 93921
Honey Jones, Innkeeper

Victorian Inn on the Park

Victoriana lives in San Francisco! Overlooking Golden Gate Park, this 1897 registered historic landmark inn has been carefully restored and furnished. An evening sip of wine in the parlor, home-baked breads for breakfast, along with friendly conversation among guests and the innkeepers, are a few of the attractions at this centrally located inn.

 12 rooms, $78/$138 B&B
 2 suites, $128/$245 B&B
Visa, MC, Amex

all private baths

open year-round

 children over 5
no pets

 Golden Gate Park, Japanese Tea Gardens, De Young Museum

breakfast
complimentary wine

no smoking in dining room

From S.F. airport, Hwy. 101 (N) towards Golden Gate Bridge, exit Fell St. for 1 mi. Turn R. on Lyon St.

415-931-1830
301 Lyon St., San Francisco, CA 94117
Lisa & William Benau, Innkeepers

Villa Royale Inn

Easy, casual, and unpretentious is this luxurious inn in glamorous Palm Springs. Ranged around flower-filled courtyards with fountains and two swimming pools, rooms decorated with furnishings and treasures from around the world have their own private gardens and patios. International-style dinners are presented in the romantic dining room.

 4 rooms, $65/$95 B&B
27 suites & villas, $120/$325 B&B
Visa, MC, Amex

all private baths; 6 Jacuzzis

open year-round

 children 18 or over
no pets

pool, spas, bikes, in-room movies, golf, tennis, Mt. San Jacinto tram, shopping

complimentary breakfast
dinner
wine available

smoking accepted

wheelchair access (4 rooms)
conference facilities (75)

Exit I-10 at Rte. 111. Continue 9 mi. and turn L. onto Indian Trail.

619-327-2314
1620 So. Indian Ave., Palm Springs, CA 92264
Charles Murawski & Bob Lee, Innkeepers

The Wine Country Inn

Unparalleled comfort and privacy give this inn, surrounded by wildflowers and colorful plantings and perched on a knoll overlooking the manicured vineyards and nearby hills of Napa Valley, a special atmosphere of intimacy and ease. Some guest rooms boast fireplaces and balconies; all are decorated with local antiques and family-made quilts.

 22 rooms, $88/$151 B&B
3 suites, $138/$172 B&B
Visa, MC

all private baths

closed Dec. 18 to Dec. 26

 children not encouraged
no pets

 pool & Jacuzzi, wineries, tennis, golf, hiking

breakfast

smoking accepted

 wheelchair access

From S.F. take I-80 (N) to Napa exit. Follow Hwy. 29 (N) 18 mi. to St. Helena & 2 mi. beyond to Lodi Lane. Turn R. for .3 mi. to inn.

707-963-7077
1152 Lodi Lane, St. Helena, CA 94574
Jim Smith, Innkeeper

COLORADO

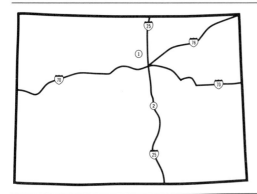

Briar Rose Bed & Breakfast, Boulder   1
Hearthstone Inn, Colorado Springs   2

Briar Rose Bed & Breakfast Inn

Roses, fruit, and down puffs in the guest rooms are only part of the welcome at this small beautiful rose-colored brick inn, with its Queen Anne shingles on the second story. An ideal climate and nearby mountains offer myriad diversions, including climbing, hiking, bicycling, running, cross-country skiing, and some of the best downhill skiing in the world.

 11 rooms, $68/$98 B&B
Visa, MC, Amex, Diners

 breakfast
dinner available upon request
sherry available

6 private, 2½ shared baths

smoking accepted

open year-round

 children accepted
pets accepted in specific rooms

 golf, swimming, hiking, biking, skiing, health club

Take Hwy. 36 (N) which becomes 28th St. Turn L. at Arapahoe St. (2nd light). Continue (W) to 22nd St. & turn R. Inn is on corner.

303-442-3007
2151 Arapahoe Ave., Boulder, CO 80302
Emily Hunter, Innkeeper

Hearthstone Inn

A whimsical rainbow of grey, lavender, lilac, peach, plum, and magenta mark the authentically painted exterior of the buildings of this Victorian inn. Wonderful antiques, including a piano and an oaken pump organ, color-coordinated linens in intriguing guest rooms, gourmet breakfasts, and a friendly, helpful staff make this a welcome respite from the world.

 25 rooms, $68/$99 B&B
Visa, MC, Amex

breakfast; banquets
and picnics arranged

23 private, 1 shared baths

non-smokers preferred

open year-round

 conference facilities (25)

 children accepted
no pets

 croquet, puzzles, games, walking, golf, tennis, museums, rafting, Pikes Peak

From I-25, Exit 143 (Uintah St.) (E) away from mountains 3 blocks to Cascade. Turn R. (S) 7 blocks to corner of Cascade & St. Vrain.

719-473-4413 or 800-521-1885
506 No. Cascade Ave., Colorado Springs, CO 80903
Dot Williams, Innkeeper

 Rates are quoted for 2 people for 1 night and do not necessarily include service charges and state taxes. For more detailed information, ask the inns for their brochures.

AP — American Plan (3 meals included in room rate)

MAP — Modified American Plan (breakfast & dinner included in room rate)

EP — European Plan (meals not included in room rate)

B&B — Bed & Breakfast (breakfast included in room rate)

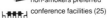 — represents recreational facilities and diversions either on the premises of an inn or nearby

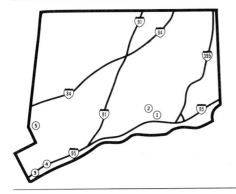

Bee and Thistle Inn, Old Lyme   1
Griswold Inn, Essex   2
Homestead Inn, Greenwich   3
Silvermine Tavern, Norwalk   4
West Lane Inn, Ridgefield   5

Bee and Thistle Inn

In an unspoiled historic village on the Lieutenant River, this lovely 1756 inn reflects a gracious lifestyle, with its English gardens, many fireplaces, sunlit porches, beautiful, carved staircase, canopied and 4-poster beds, antique quilts, and furnishings. Widely commended for its cuisine, it has been called a most romantic place to dine.

 11 rooms, $62/$105 EP
Visa, MC, Amex, Diners

 9 private, 1 shared baths

 closed Jan. 1 to Jan. 14

 children over 11
no pets

bikes, gardens, river, museums, art, beach, golf, Mystic

 breakfast, lunch, dinner,
Sun. brunch, English tea
wine & liquor available

smoking in parlors only

 conference facilities (20)

I-95 (S) Exit 70, turn R. off ramp to inn, 3rd bldg. on L. I-95 (N) Exit 70, turn L. off ramp to 1st light, R. to next light, then L. to inn, 3rd bldg. on L.

203-434-1667
100 Lyme St., Old Lyme, CT 06371
Bob & Penny Nelson, Innkeepers

The Griswold Inn

A kaleidoscope of nostalgic images delights the eye here: myriad Currier & Ives steamboat prints and Antonio Jacobsen marine art, ship models, firearms, a potbellied stove, to name a few. The superb New England cuisine features seafood, prime rib, meat pies, and the inn's own 1776 sausages. Lucius Beebe considered the Taproom the most handsome in America.

 14 rooms, $75 B&B
9 suites, $85/$165 B&B
Visa, MC, Amex

 all private baths

 dining room closed Christmas
Eve/Day

children accepted

tennis, golf, swimming, Goodspeed Opera, Mystic Seaport

 breakfast, lunch, dinner
famous Sun. Hunt Breakfast
wine & liquor available

 conference facilities (20)

I-91 (S) to Exit 22 (S). Rte. 9 (S) to Exit 3 Essex. I-95 (N&S) to Exit 69 to Rte. 9 (N) to Exit 3 Essex.

203-767-1812
36 Main St., Essex, CT 06426
Victoria & William Winterer, Innkeepers

The Homestead Inn

Gracious, historic elegance combined with a relaxed, convivial atmosphere and the superlative talents of Parisian chef, Jacques Thiebeult, attracts guests from far and wide to the Homestead Inn, set among noble trees in a beautiful, quiet residential area, 45 minutes from New York City. The exquisitely decorated and appointed rooms and popular restaurant are much in demand, so reserve early.

 13 rooms, $82/$150 B&B
6 suites, $135/$165 B&B
Visa, MC, Amex, Diners

 all private baths

 open all year

 children accepted
no pets

 breakfast, lunch, dinner
wine & liquor available

 smoking allowed

 conference facilities (14)

In Greenwich I-95, Exit 3 (Arch St.) L. at end of ramp to 2nd light and L. at Horse Neck Lane to L. at Field Point Rd. Continue ¼ mi. to inn on R.

203-869-7500
420 Field Point Rd., Greenwich, CT 06830
Lessie Davison & Nancy Smith, Innkeepers

The Silvermine Tavern

A 1785 inn beside a millpond with swans and a waterfall—what could be more romantic? Early American guest rooms, a treasure house of Early Americana and primitive paintings, and country dining at its best, with such New England dishes as lobster pie and Indian pudding, are just a few of the inducements here.

10 rooms, $74/$80 B&B
Visa, MC, Amex, Diners

all private baths

closed Tues., exc. June, July, Aug.

children accepted
no pets

golf, boating, beach, tennis

complimentary breakfast
lunch, dinner, Sun. brunch
wine & liquor available

non-smoking dining area

conference facilities (40)

I-95, Exit 15 or Merrit Pkwy. Exit 39.
Call for directions.

203-847-4558
Perry Ave., Norwalk, CT 06850
Francis C. Whitman, Innkeeper

West Lane Inn

Rich oak paneling, deep pile carpeting, and a cheery fire crackling on the hearth sets the tone of polished refinement at this luxurious inn. Framed by a stand of majestic old maples, a broad lawn, and flowering shrubs, it offers gracious hospitality and a quiet retreat from worldly cares, about an hour north of New York City.

20 rooms, $90/$120 B&B
fireplaces, $150
Visa, MC, Amex, Diners

all private baths

open year-round

children accepted
no pets

golf, tennis, xc skiing, swimming

breakfast & light lunch

smoking allowed

wheelchair access (1 room)
conference facilities (18)

From NYC & Westside Hwy. (N) to Sawmill River Pkwy. & Exit 6 (Katonah). Turn R. on Rte. 35 (E) 12 mi. to Ridgefield. Inn is on L. From Rte. 90 & I-84, Exit 3 to Rte. 7 (S) to Rte. 35 and Ridgefield.

203-438-7323
22 West Lane, Ridgefield, CT 06877
Maureen Mayer, Innkeeper

What Is The Independent Innkeepers' Association?

As mentioned in our tribute to Norman Simpson, this association had its earliest beginnings in the late '60s, when in the course of some informal dinner gatherings attended by the inns featured in his book, Country Inns and Back Roads, *Norman discovered that country inn- keepers felt isolated and out of contact with like-minded people in the hospitality industry. Hotel and motel organizations catered to commercially oriented establishments, and offered little of value to keepers of country inns. Their appreciation and need for gathering together with other innkeepers was immediately obvious.*

The opportunity to discuss mutual problems and find solutions, and the discovery that their failures and triumphs were shared by others, gave rise to the idea of a network of fine country inns in which was implicit the sense of responsibility to each other and their shared values and standards in serving the public.

Norman began holding annual meetings, which would take place at one or another of the inns in this book. Then, the need for smaller, more focused sessions resulted in several regional meetings in various parts of the country throughout the year. Norman's travels had taken him far afield of New England, and "his" inns were scattered throughout the United States and into parts of Canada.

By 1972, he formally established this loose collection of inns as the Independent Inn- keepers' Association. The innkeepers in this group came from all walks of life, many of them having left successful careers and lucrative opportunities to experience the joys and tribula- tions of innkeeping. An important quality in each of them was not only a deep sense of commitment to their inns, but also an enthusiasm and desire to be involved with other inn- keepers who shared their goals and standards and who wanted to work together for the common good.

In addition to workshops and discussions dealing with the many problems that beset any business, the examples and stories of particular successes in various areas provide members with new ideas and fresh incentives.

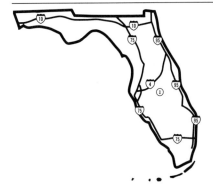

Chalet Suzanne, Lake Wales   1

Chalet Suzanne

"Fairy tales can come true . . ." or perhaps it's more like the Arabian Nights. This is a storybook inn with an around-the-world look to its many cottages grouped at odd angles, its fountain courtyards, and its fascinating furnishings. The award-winning restaurant is famous for its gourmet fare.

26 rooms, $85/$155 EP
4 suites, $95/$155 EP
Visa, MC, Amex, Discov

all private baths

restaurant closed Mon.;
Tues. A.M., May—Dec.

children accepted
$20 per pet

gardens, pool,
central Florida attractions
golf, tennis nearby

breakfast, lunch, & dinner
special MAP pkg. May thru Nov.
lounge

smoking accepted

wheelchair access (1 room)
conference facilities (60)

I-4 (W) from Orlando to U.S. Hwy.
27; L. on U.S. 27 (S), 18 mi. Turn
L. on County Rd. 17A for 1.5 mi. to
inn on R.

813-676-6011 or 800-288-6011
U.S. Hwy. 27 & County Rd. 17A, P.O. Drawer AC,
Lake Wales, FL 33859-9003
The Hinshaw Family, Innkeepers

The feeling of fellowship and family is a strong bond rooted in the shared purpose of maintaining what is finest and best in the true tradition and spirit of American innkeeping.

Today, a year after Norman Simpson's death, the board of directors and the membership are continuing and expanding the work he began. In this ever-increasingly competitive arena, we will hold to the standards of personal hospitality, which he defined and which are so important to us and our many guests who look for both professional excellence and a genuine feeling of friendly welcome. We do indeed see ourselves as "a bright lantern shining in the dark night, offering warm hospitality and sustenance to our guests."

Some Criteria For Membership In The IIA

These are a few of the criteria used in evaluating the eligibility of an inn for membership in the IIA. Other more stringent criteria are also used; however, these are the most basic requirements.

Inn is owner-operated or the innkeeper/manager is highly committed to the spirit of personal hospitality. Staff shows genuine interest toward guests.

The innkeepers has owned/run the inn for a minimum of 3 years, or, if from a background of successful innkeeping, 2 years.

Inn building is architecturally interesting and attractive with appropriately groomed grounds, tasteful, comfortable, and inviting interior furnishings, and at least one common room for houseguests only. Guest rooms are attractively and completely furnished for comfort of guests.

Housekeeping and maintenance is excellent, with immaculate guest rooms and bathrooms.

Dining room provides pleasant dining experience with quality food, excellent service, and attractive decor.

Gastonian, The, Savannah   2
Greyfield Inn, Cumberland Island   3
Veranda, The, Senoia   1

The Gastonian

Stunning is probably the best word to describe the decoration and the hospitality at this most elegant southern Colonial inn (two 1868 mansions linked by a beautiful garden courtyard) in the largest historic landmark district in the U.S. Exquisite antiques, working fireplaces, luxurious bathtubs, service and attention *extraordinaire* await the pampered guest here.

 10 rooms, $95/$150 B&B
3 suites, $150/$225 B&B
Visa, MC, Amex

all private baths, 6 Jacuzzis

open year-round

 children over 12
no pets

hot tub on sun deck;
tennis, golf, deep-sea fishing
central A/C, cable/color TV

full breakfast
wine available

smoking discouraged

wheelchair access (1 room)
conference facilities (25)

From I-16 exit at W. Broad St. straight ahead with no turns, which becomes Gaston St. Continue to inn at 220 East Gaston St.

912-232-2869
220 E. Gaston St., Savannah, GA 31401
Hugh & Roberta Lineberger, Innkeepers

Greyfield Inn

This turn-of-the-century mansion is on Cumberland Island, Georgia's largest and southernmost island. Miles of hiking trails traverse the island's unique ecosystems along with a beautiful, endless beach for shelling, swimming, and sunning. Excellent birdwatching, too. Fine food, lovely original furnishings, and a peaceful, relaxing environment provide guests with a step back into another era.

 7 rooms, $180 AP
2 suites, $200 AP
Visa, MC, personal checks

1 private, 3 shared baths

open year-round

 children accepted
no pets

birdwatching, hiking, swimming,
shelling, biking, fishing,
photography

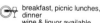 breakfast, picnic lunches,
dinner
wine & liquor available

smoking allowed in bar

 conference facilities (18)

Cumberland Island is accessible only by boat or plane; 2 ferry services provide transp. to Island from Fernandina, FL or St. Mary's, GA.

904-261-6408
Cumberland Island, GA/P.O. Drawer B,
Fernandina Beach, FL 32034
Oliver & Mary Jo Ferguson, Innkeepers

The Veranda

This elegantly restored turn-of-the century inn on the National Register of Historic Places, comfortably furnished in period antiques, offers guests a quiet, relaxed Southern lifestyle. A treasury of books, games, puzzles, and the broad rocking-chair veranda, which gives the inn its name, along with gourmet meals and lavish breakfasts are only some of the enjoyments to be had here.

 9 rooms, $65/$85 B&B
Visa, MC

all private baths, 1 whirlpool

open year-round
reservations necessary

 children accepted (inquire)
no pets

player piano/organ, library,
games, kaleidoscopes, historic
touring, antiquing, tennis, golf

 breakfast
dinner & lunch by reservation only

limited smoking

 wheelchair access (downstairs)
conference facilities (20)

From Atlanta I-85 (S), Exit 12; L. (SE) on Hwy. 74 for 16.7 mi. R. (S) on Rockaway Rd. for 3.3 mi. At light turn L. (E) for 1 block to inn.

404-599-3905
252 Seavy St., Senoia, GA 30276
Jan & Bobby Boal, Innkeepers

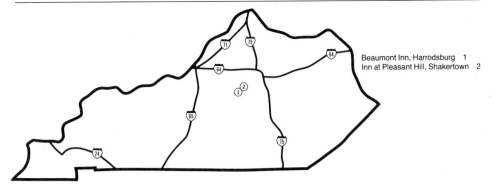

Beaumont Inn, Harrodsburg   1
Inn at Pleasant Hill, Shakertown   2

Beaumont Inn

606-734-3381
638 Beaumont Dr., Harrodsburg, KY 40330
The Dedman Family, Innkeepers

Owned and operated by four generations of the Dedman family, this country inn, on the National Register of Historic Places, was built in 1845 as a school for young ladies. In the heart of Bluegrass country, it is redolent of Southern history, brimming with beautiful antiques, fascinating memorabilia, and the food is traditional Kentucky fare. Over 30 varieties of trees grace the grounds.

 29 rooms, $55/$85 EP
Visa, MC, Amex

 all private baths

 closed mid-Dec. to mid-March

children accepted
no pets

swimming pool, tennis, shuffleboard, golf, fishing, historic
attractions

 breakfast, lunch, dinner
BYOB

 conference facilities (25)

In Harrodsburg at intersection with U.S. 68, take U.S. 127 (S) to inn, at south end of town on east side of U.S. 127.

Inn at Pleasant Hill

606-734-5411
3500 Lexington Rd., Harrodsburg, KY 40330
Ann Voris, Innkeeper

Part of a restored Shaker community, originally established in 1805, the inn's rooms are located in 15 of the 30 original buildings clustered along a country road on 2700 acres in Bluegrass country. Rooms are simply and beautifully furnished with examples of Shaker crafts, meals are hearty and homemade, and tours, demonstrations, and cultural events abound.

 76 rooms, $44/$70 EP
5 suites, $65/$100 EP

 all private baths

 closed Dec. 24 & 25

children accepted
no pets in dining room bldg.

village touring, riverboat

 breakfast, lunch, dinner

 conference facilities (75)

From Lexington, U.S. 68 (W) 25 mi. and R. to village. From Harrodsburg, U.S. 68 (E) 7 mi. Turn L. to village.

Rates are quoted for 2 people for 1 night and do not necessarily include service charges and state taxes. For more detailed information, ask the inns for their brochures.

AP — American Plan (3 meals included in room rate)

MAP — Modified American Plan (breakfast & dinner included in room rate)

EP — European Plan (meals not included in room rate)

B&B — Bed & Breakfast (breakfast included in room rate)

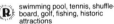 — represents recreational facilities and diversions either on the premises of an inn or nearby

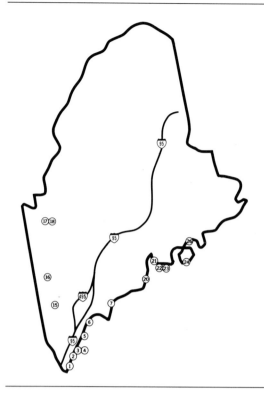

Black Point Inn, Prouts Neck   5
Captain Lord Mansion, Kennebunkport   3
Charmwoods, Naples   15
Claremont Hotel and Cottages, Southwest Harbor   24
Country Club Inn, Rangeley   17
Crocker House Country Inn, Hancock Point   26
Dockside Guest Quarters, York   1
Goose Cove Lodge, Deer Isle   22
Hartwell House, Ogunquit   2
Homewood Inn, Yarmouth   6
Old Fort Inn, Kennebunkport   4
Pentagoet Inn, Castine   21
Pilgrim's Inn, Deer Isle   23
Rangeley Inn, Rangeley   18
Squire Tarbox Inn, Westport Island   7
Waterford Inne, East Waterford   16
Whitehall Inn, Camden   20

Black Point Inn

Quintessentially New England is this seaside resort inn, the favored retreat of generations of guests since the late 1900s. Easy, gracious hospitality and understated, genteel elegance, along with the vast ocean views, bracing salt air, hearty meals, beachcombing, sailing, and more, make this a world-class seaside resort-inn.

75 rooms, $200/$300 AP
5 suites, $270/$330 AP
Visa, MC, Amex

all private baths

closed Nov. 1 to May 1

children over 8
no pets

 indoor/outdoor pool/Jacuzzi, putting green, croquet, golf, tennis

breakfast, lunch, dinner
wine & liquor available

no smoking in dining room

conference facilities

I-95 (N) to Exit 5 and U.S. Rte. 1, 10 mi. (N). Turn R. on Rte. 207, 4.5 mi. to inn. Or, I-95 (S) to Exit 7; R. at Scarborough Old Orchard (Rte. 1). L. at 2nd light onto Rte. 7 as above.

207-883-4126
510 Black Point Rd., Prouts Neck, ME 04074
Normand H. Dugas, Innkeeper

Captain Lord Mansion

The beautifully appointed, spacious rooms of this stately 1812 mansion, with its elliptical staircase and imposing cupola, feature period wallpapers, crystal chandeliers, working fireplaces, and many objets d'art. The superb comfort and gracious hospitality have been rewarded for many years with 4 diamonds by AAA. Many year-round activities are offered in this charming seacoast village.

22 rooms, $69/$159 B&B
2 suites, $199/$299 B&B
Visa, MC, Discov

all private baths; 4 Jacuzzis

open year-round

children over 12
no pets

 antiquing, shopping, beaches, sailing, whale-watching

full breakfast
BYOB

smoking in guest rooms only

conference facilities (15)

ME Tpke., Exit 3. L. onto Rte. 35 for 5.5 mi. to Rte. 9 (E). Turn L., go over bridge, R. onto Ocean Ave.; after ³⁄₁₀ mi., turn L. onto Green St.

207-967-3141
P.O. Box 800, Kennebunkport, ME 04046
Bev Davis & Rick Litchfield, Innkeepers

Charmwoods

Enjoying the magnificent lake and mountain views from the gracious, commodious living room, with its massive fieldstone fireplace, is like being a guest at a house party. There are a number of intriguing conversation pieces. This lakeside/countryside retreat offers both indoor and outdoor diversions—bathing, boating, canoeing, fishing, and tennis, to name a few.

 3 rooms, $95/$105 B&B
2 suites, $95/$105 B&B
no credit cards

 all private baths

 closed late Oct. to mid-June

 children over 11
no pets

swimming, fishing, tennis, canoeing, shuffleboard, golf, horseback riding, bicycling

 breakfast

no smoking in bedrooms

I-95 Exit 8 (Portland-Westbrook) & R. on Riverside St. 1 mi. to L. turn on Rte. 302. (W) & 30 mi. to Naples. Inn is just beyond village on R.

207-693-6798
Route 302, P.O. Box 217, Naples, ME 04055
Bill & Marilyn Lewis, Innkeepers

Claremont Hotel & Cottages

The dock and the Boathouse on Somes Sound are the center of much activity at this 105-year-old summer hotel, although croquet and the annual Claremont Classic run them a close second. On the National Register of Historic Places, the Claremont, with its panoramic views of mountains and ocean, offers serene and happy sojourns to its many returning guests.

 8 rooms, $130/$140 MAP
16 suites/cottages, $110/$155 MAP
no credit cards

 mostly private baths

cottages closed 10/16—5/22; hotel, 9/17—6/15

 children accepted
no pets

tennis, croquet, rowboats, bikes, golf, sailing, swimming, Acadia Nat'l Park

 breakfast and dinner; lunch mid-July and Aug. only. EP off-season wine & liquor available

no smoking in guest rooms

wheelchair access (4 cottages)
conference facilities (125)

ME Tpke., Exit 15 (Augusta). Rte. 3 (E) thru Ellsworth to Mt. Desert Is. Take Rte. 102 to SW Harbor. Follow signs.

207-244-5036
Box 137, Southwest Harbor, ME 04679
John Madeira, Jr., Manager

Country Club Inn

Few locations offer such beauty and grandeur in all seasons as Rangeley, Maine, with its wide skies, vast mountain ranges, and sparkling lake. This magnificent scenery can be enjoyed from the guest rooms, dining room, and lounge of 2,000-foot-high Country Club Inn, in the heart of fishing, hiking, and skiing country.

 19 rooms, $126/$146 MAP
Visa, MC, Amex

 all private baths

 closed Nov. & April

 children accepted
pets accepted

pool, golf, hiking, skiing, xc skiing, snowmobiling

 breakfast & dinner
wine, beer, & liquor available

smoking in designated area

 conference facilities (125)

ME Tpke., Exit 12 to Rte. 4. I-91 in VT & NH to St. Johnsbury; (E) on Rte. 2 to Gorham & Rte. 16 (N) to Rangeley.

207-864-3831
P.O. Box 680, Rangeley, ME 04970
Sue Crory & Family, Innkeepers

Crocker House Country Inn

Quiet and sequestered, this pleasant inn sits on Hancock Point, a 3-minute walk from the ocean, 4 clay tennis courts, and the town dock, where moorings are available for seafaring guests. Built in 1884, the inn was carefully restored in 1986, and now provides bright, cheerful lodgings, extraordinary cuisine with garden-fresh vegetables, and a soothing, peaceful atmosphere.

 9 rooms, $50/$68 B&B
1 suite, $50/$75 B&B
Visa, MC, Amex

 all private baths

 closed Jan. 1—Apr. 20;
M-W in Nov. & Dec.

 children with prior permission
pets with prior permission

library, tennis, touring, Acadia Nat'l. Park, ocean, antiquing

 breakfast & dinner
Sun. brunch
wine & liquor

no smoking in dining room

 conference facilities (36)

From Ellsworth on U.S. Rte. 1 go 7.9 mi. (N) to R. at Hancock Pt. Rd. Continue 5 mi. to inn on R.

207-422-6806
Hancock, ME 04640
Richard Malaby, Innkeeper

Dockside Guest Quarters

This small resort on a private peninsula in York Harbor offers a panorama of ocean and harbor activities. The early Maine seacoast homestead and adjacent buildings contain attractive guest rooms and suites with rambling porches where guests relax and enjoy the water views. A marina is on the premises, with an ocean beach nearby. The York historic district is within walking distance.

 15 rooms, $46/$78 EP
6 suites, $83/$110 EP
Visa, MC (under $100)

 19 private, 1 shared baths

closed Oct. 23 to May 1

children welcome
pets accepted with restrictions

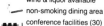 boat rentals, fishing, shuffleboard, badminton, croquet, swimming, golf, tennis, outlet shopping, historic sites

breakfast, lunch, dinner
AP available
wine & liquor available

non-smoking dining area

conference facilities (30)

From I-95 exit to U.S. 1 and Rte. 1-A thru Old York to Rte. 103. Cross bridge & watch for signs to inn.

207-363-2868
Harris Island Rd., P.O. Box 205, York, ME 03909
Eric, David, & Harriette Lusty, Innkeepers

Goose Cove Lodge

This rustic and comfortable lodge is on a secluded peaceful cove where pine trees and rock ledges meet the ocean. Cottages have fireplaces, sundecks, and wonderful views. Pleasant day trips on land and water, evening entertainment, natural beauty, lobster cookouts and other good cuisine offer refreshment of body and spirit to guests of all ages.

 8 rooms, $120/$145 MAP
13 cottages, $145/$180 MAP
personal checks accepted

all private baths

closed mid-Oct. to April 30

children accepted
no pets

 nature trails, beach, canoe, golf, sailing, Acadia Nat'l Park

breakfast & dinner, high season
continental breakfast, low season
BYOB

no smoking in dining room

wheelchair access (1 room)
conference facilities

I-95 to Augusta, Rte. 3 to Belfast, Rte. 1 (N), 4 mi. past Bucksport, R. on Rte. 15. In town of Deer Isle R. on Sunset Rd., 3 mi. to inn sign & R. 1.5 mi. to inn.

207-348-2508
Deer Isle, Sunset, ME 04683
Elli and George Pavloff, Innkeepers

Hartwell House

Sculpted flower gardens color the view from the balcony rooms overlooking the lawn sloping down to the river at this sophisticated inn. Early American and English antiques, stunning pastel fabrics, and fresh flowers add to the country house atmosphere. Within an easy walk is the wonderful Marginal Way and Perkins Cove.

 11 rooms, $65/$135 B&B
5 suites, $100/$175 B&B
Visa, MC, Amex

all private baths

closed 2nd & 3rd wks. in Jan.

children over 14
no pets

 Atlantic Ocean, beach, fishing, swimming, golf, tennis, xc skiing, biking

breakfast
wine available

no smoking

conference facilities (10)

I-95 (N) & York/Ogunquit Exit. L. on Rte. 1 for 4.4 mi. to R. at Pine Hill Rd. L. at Shore Rd. for .2 mi. to inn.

207-646-7210
116 Shore Rd., P.O. Box 393, Ogunquit, ME 03907
Trisha & Jim Hartwell, Innkeepers

Homewood Inn on Casco Bay

A rambling colony of cottages and buildings along the rocky shore and among the woods and fields bordering Casco Bay, this resort-inn has a homelike, comfortable feeling. Wednesday night clambakes, home-cooked breakfasts, fresh air, and the natural beauty add to the friendly atmosphere, Historic, scenic, and shopping attractions abound.

 25 rooms, $53/$94 EP
15 cottages, $125/$235 EP
Visa, MC, Amex

all private baths

open year-round

children accepted
small dogs by prior arrangement

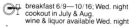 pool, tennis, croquet, ocean bathing, golf, boating, riding, state parks

breakfast 6/9—10/16; Wed. night cookout in July & Aug.
wine & liquor available Wed. night

wheelchair access (some rooms)

I-95 Exit 9 to Rte. 1 (N). Turn R. at Mobil station in Yarmouth & follow signs (3 mi.) to inn.

207-846-3351
Drinkwater Point, P.O. Box 196, Yarmouth, ME 04096
The Websters & Gillettes, Innkeepers

Old Fort Inn

A short walk from the ocean along a country road, this secluded inn in an old seaport town offers rooms with antiques, canopied and 4-poster beds, and color TV. Guests find new friends over a buffet breakfast of fresh fruit and homemade breads; a charming antiques shop, fresh-water pool, and private tennis court provide pleasant diversion.

 14 rooms, $90/$140 B&B
2 suites, $148/$195 B&B
Visa, MC, Amex, Discov

 all private baths; 4 Jacuzzis

closed Dec. 10—April

children over 12 accepted
no pets

 tennis court, pool, bikes, ocean,
golf, walking, jogging

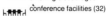 breakfast

smoking discouraged

conference facilities (32)

I-95 Exit 3, turn L. on Rte. 35 for 5.5 mi. L. at light at Sunoco station for .3 mi. to Ocean Ave. Go .9 mi. to Colony Hotel, then L. & follow signs .3 mi. to inn.

207-967-5353
Old Fort Ave., P.O. Box M, Kennebunkport, ME 04046
Sheila & David Aldrich, Innkeepers

The Pentagöet Inn

Capacious porches, fresh flowers, nightly room freshening are a few of the "perks" at this lovely old Victorian inn, with its feeling of a private country home and its excellent food and extensive wine list. Tiny, historic Castine in Penobscot Bay offers fresh sea air, harbor activities and a tranquil setting.

 16 rooms, $145/$160 MAP
1 suite, $185 MAP
Visa, MC; personal checks preferred

 all private baths

 closed Dec. thru March

 children over 12
no pets

tennis, golf
boating, hiking, biking,

 breakfast & dinner;
to the public by reservation
wine & liquor available

 no smoking

I-95 to Augusta & Rte. 3 (E) to Belfast, turn L. (N) on Rte. 1 past Bucksport 3 mi. to R. (S) on Rte. 175. Turn (S) on Rte. 166 to Castine. Inn is on Main St.

207-326-8616
Main St., P.O. Box 4, Castine, ME 04421
Lindsey & Virginia Miller, Innkeepers

Pilgrim's Inn

Overlooking Northwest Harbor and a picturesque millpond, this rambling 1793 Colonial home is surrounded by the unspoiled beauty of remote Deer Isle in Penobscot Bay. Glowing hearths, soft Colonial colors, pumpkin pine floors, antique furnishings, combined with warm hospitality and gourmet meals in the charming barn dining room, have pleased many happy and contented guests.

 13 rooms, $130/$150 MAP
1 cottage, $180 MAP
no credit cards

 private & shared baths

 open mid-May to mid-Oct.

 children over 10 accepted
no pets

 touring, hiking, bicycling, sailing,
golf, tennis

 breakfast and dinner
wine & liquor available

 smoking in common rooms only

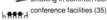 conference facilities (35)

I-95 (N) to Augusta. Rte. 3 (N) to Belfast, thru Bucksport to Rte. 15 (S), thru Blue Hill. Over bridge to Deer Isle Village. Turn R., 1 block to inn on left.

207-348-6615
Deer Isle, ME 04627
Dud and Jean Hendrick, Innkeepers

Rangeley Inn

The big blue clapboard building with the long veranda across the front has that grand old summer hotel look and the homelike, roomy lobby has a bit of an old-fashioned feeling. However, the elegant dining room is up to the minute with creative, interesting menus. Several acres of lawns and gardens border a bird sanctuary, and the area is a nature-lover's and sportsman's paradise.

 50 rooms, $59/$95 EP
1 suite, $95 EP
Visa, MC, Amex

all private baths; several whirlpools

open year-round

children accepted

 moose-watching, touring,
antiques, swimming, boating,
hiking, downhill & xc skiing

 breakfast & dinner; MAP optional
dining closed 4/15—5/15; early
Dec.; wine & liquor available

limited smoking in dining room

 wheelchair access (1 room)
conference facilities (150)

On Rte. 4 past Farmington 40 mi. to Rangeley. From west take Rte. 16. Inn is on Main St.

207-864-3341 or 5641
Box 398, Main St., Rangeley, ME 04970
Fay & Ed Carpenter, Innkeepers

The Squire Tarbox Inn

This handsome antique farmhouse on a wooded hillside by a small inlet, offers historical significance, a natural country setting, relaxed comfort and a diversity of Main Coast interests. Quiet rural privacy is here for guests who seek moments of personal solitude. Known for its savory fireside dinners and goat cheese from its purebred dairy herd.

 11 rooms, $100/$160 MAP
Visa, MC, Amex

 all private baths

closed late Oct. to mid-May

children over 14
no pets

 walking path, rowboat on premises, beaches, harbors, antiques nearby

breakfast for guests only; dinner to public by reservation wine & liquor available

smoking in limited area

I-95 to Brunswick, Exit 22, follow Rte. 1 (N) past Bath bridge 7 mi. to Rte. 144. Continue 8.5 mi. on Westport Island.

207-882-7693
R.R. 2, Box 620, Route 144, Wiscasset, ME 04578
Bill and Karen Mitman, Innkeepers

The Waterford Inne

Combining their considerable talents in hospitality and the domestic arts, Rosalie and Barbara Vanderzanden have made a very special inn out of the handsome farmhouse they have lovingly restored and furnished. Their attention to detail is apparent in beautifully decorated rooms and in the imaginative meals served on china from their 'round-the-world collection.

 9 rooms, $55/$85 EP
1 suite, $85 EP
no credit cards

7 private baths; 1 shared bath

closed March, April, Thanksgiving wk.

children accepted
pets accepted

 library, parlor games, downhill & xc skiing, swimming, boating, hiking, antiquing

 breakfast & dinner
BYOB

smoking accepted

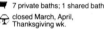 conference facilities (15)

I-95, Exit 11, to Rte. 26 (N) for 28 mi. to Norway. L. fork on Rte. 118W for 9 mi. L. on Rte. 37S for .6 mi. Turn R. past store .5 mi. to inn.

207-583-4037
Box 49 Chadbourne Rd., East Waterford, ME 04233
Rosalie & Barbara Vanderzanden, Innkeepers

Whitehall Inn

If ever an inn and a setting were made for each other, this is it. Tree-lined streets, comfortable old homes echo the feeling of old-fashioned friendliness and hospitality in this rambling, homey inn, originally built in 1834, and operating as an inn since 1901. The inn has been run by the Dewing family for 19 years.

 50 rooms, $100/$140 MAP
Visa, MC

private & shared baths

closed Oct. 15 to May 26

children accepted
no pets

 tennis, shuffleboard, gardens, library, games, rocking chairs, golf, state park, lakes, sailing

breakfast & dinner
wine & liquor available

 no smoking in dining room

Camden is 2 hrs. north of Portland on Rte. 1. Inn is .5 mi. north of village.

207-236-3391
52 High St., P.O. Box 558, Camden, ME 04843
The Dewing Family, Innkeepers

Rates are quoted for 2 people for 1 night and do not necessarily include service charges and state taxes. For more detailed information, ask the inns for their brochures.

AP — American Plan (3 meals included in room rate)

MAP — Modified American Plan (breakfast & dinner included in room rate)

EP — European Plan (meals not included in room rate)

B&B — Bed & Breakfast (breakfast included in room rate)

R — represents recreational facilities and diversions either on the premises of an inn or nearby

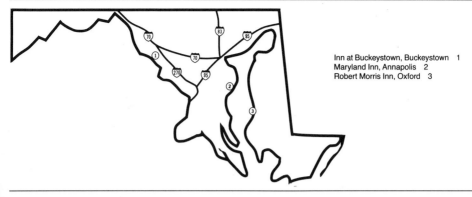

Inn at Buckeystown, Buckeystown 1
Maryland Inn, Annapolis 2
Robert Morris Inn, Oxford 3

The Inn at Buckeystown

Lovingly restored and converted, this impressive 1897 Victorian mansion and 1884 church are in a nostalgic village, on the National Register of Historic Places. Rooms are elegantly and luxuriously furnished with outstanding antiques and collectibles. A wraparound porch with rockers looks out on parklike grounds. Gourmet dining and the friendly ambience bring guests back again and again.

  8 rooms, $110/$175 MAP
1 suite, $200/$350 MAP
Visa, MC

 private & shared baths

 open year-round

 children over 16
no pets

 lawn games on premises,
hiking, antiquing, Civil War sites

 breakfast & dinner
complimentary wine

 no smoking in dining rooms

conference facilities (20)

From I-70 or I-270, take Rte. 85 (S) to Buckeystown. Inn is on left. (35 mi. from Dulles Airport.)

301-874-5755
3521 Buckeystown Pike, Buckeystown, MD 21717-9999
Dan Pelz, Owner; Rebecca Shipman, Innkeeper

Maryland Inn—Historic Inns of Annapolis

Gracefully situated in the heart of the 18th-century historic district near Chesapeake Bay, the Maryland Inn is handsomely restored and furnished with antiques and reproductions. The award-winning Treaty of Paris restaurant offers marvelous Continental cuisine, and the King of France Tavern specializes in jazz entertainment.

  44 rooms, $85/$145 EP
5 suites, $135 EP
Visa, MC, Amex, Diners

 all private baths

 open year-round

 children welcome
no pets

 boating, golf, swimming
health facilities, tennis

 breakfast, lunch, dinner
Sun. brunch
wine & liquor available

smoking allowed

wheelchair access (2 rooms)
conference facilities (100)

From Baltimore, Rte. 2 to Rte. 50 (W) to 2nd Annapolis exit (Hist. Dist./Rowe Blvd.). From Washington, Rte. 50 (E) to Hist. Dist./Rowe Blvd. exit.

301-263-2641 (reservations: 800-847-8882)
16 Church Circle, Annapolis, MD 21401
Paul Pearson, Proprietor; Peg Bednarsky, Innkeeper

The Robert Morris Inn

Chesapeake Bay and the Tred Avon River play a big part in the life of this Eastern Shore country-romantic 1710 inn. Delicacies from the bay are featured in the nationally acclaimed seafood restaurant and the Tred Avon offers lovely views for many of the rooms and porches. Country furnishings add to the friendly country feeling here in the historic waterside village of Oxford.

 33 rooms, $65/$150 EP
Visa, MC, Amex

 30 private, 1 shared baths

 closed Christmas Day,
varied winter closings

 children over 10
no pets

tennis, golf, antiquing, sailing,
historic car ferry, goose hunting

 breakfast, lunch, & dinner
wine & liquor available

smoking & non-smoking rooms

 wheelchair access (2 rooms)
executive retreat (14)

Hwy. 301 to Rte. 50 (E). Turn R. on Rte. 322 for 3.4 mi. Turn R. on Rte. 333 for 9.6 mi. to inn & ferry.

301-226-5111
312 No. Morris St., P.O. Box 70, Oxford, MD 21654
Wendy & Ken Gibson, Owners; Jay Gibson, Innkeeper

MASSACHUSETTS

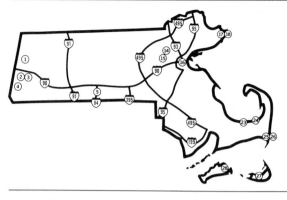

The Bramble Inn and Restaurant

Dine superbly at one of Cape Cod's top three restaurants, where Ruth Manchester creates dishes sought after by *Bon Appetit* and *Gourmet*. Wide pine floors, antiques, and flowered wallpapers adorn the guest rooms in the three 18th- and 19th-century buildings of this family-owned and operated intimate inn on the historic north side of the Cape.

 12 rooms, $75/$120 B&B
Visa, MC, Amex, Diners

 all private baths

closed Jan. 1 to April 1

 children over 8
no pets

 tennis, swimming, bicycling, horseback riding, fishing, whale-watching, antiquing

 breakfast; price-fix dinner by reservation
wine & liquor available

smoking restricted

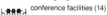 wheelchair access (3 rooms)

Rte. 6, Exit 10 & bear L. on Rte. 124 to R. on Rte. 6A for ⅛ mi. to inn on left.

508-896-7644
2019 Main St., Route 6A, Box 807, Brewster, MA 02631
Cliff & Ruth Manchester, Innkeepers

Captain's House Inn of Chatham

Complete quiet, without television, and cheerful, caring attention are here for guests who choose to stay at this historic, elegant 1839 inn set on two acres, a half-mile from Cape Cod's south shore beaches. The decor is reminiscent of Williamsburg with fine antiques, canopied beds, and fireplaces in warm, inviting guest rooms. Breakfasts with homemade granola are always a big hit.

 13 rooms, $95/$149 B&B
1 suite, $129/$149 B&B
Visa, MC, Amex

 all private baths

closed mid-Nov. to mid-Feb.

 children over 12
no pets

beaches, tennis, golf, boating, theater, fishing

breakfast
BYOB

smoking in guest rooms only

conference facilities (14)

Rte. 6 (Mid-Cape Hwy.) to Rte. 137, Exit 11 (S) to Rte. 28; L. on Rte. 28 to Chatham Center. Continue around rotary on Rte. 28 toward Orleans .5 mi. to inn on L.

508-945-0127
371 Old Harbor Rd., Chatham, Cape Cod, MA 02633
Cathy & David Eakin, Innkeepers

Charles Hinckley House

An architectural gem listed on the National Register of Historic Places on the Olde Kings Highway is this 1809 Colonial home of an early shipwright. The young innkeepers have lovingly restored and furnished it, polishing the wide pumpkin pine floors, refurbishing the fireplaces, and putting in 4-poster beds. The unspoiled natural beauty of Cape Cod Bay is just a stroll away.

 2 rooms, $98/$115 B&B
2 suites, $125/$135 B&B
personal checks accepted

 all private baths

 open year-round

 children over 10
no pets

 antiquing, historic sites, beaches, golf, tennis, sailing, fishing

 complimentary breakfast; dinner on weekends and holidays by reservation only

no smoking

 wheelchair access (1 room)

Rte. 6 (mid-Cape Hwy.) Exit 6. Turn L. onto Rte. 132 for .5 mi. Turn R. onto Rte. 6A; continue 1.5 mi. to inn.

508-362-9924
Olde Kings Hwy., (Rte. 6-A), P.O. Box 723,
Barnstable, MA 02630
Les & Miya Patrick, Innkeepers

The Charlotte Inn

Art, aesthetics, and exquisite attention to detail are the hallmarks of this beautifully restored inn, surrounded by lovely gardens along the brick pathways among the buildings. Original oils and watercolors and beautiful wallpapers adorn luxuriously furnished rooms, some with fireplaces. Cuisine at the French restaurant pleases the most sophisticated palates.

 23 rooms, $65/$295 B&B
2 suites, $275/$335 B&B
Visa, MC, Amex

 all but one private bath

 open year-round

 children over 14
no pets

boating, golfing, tennis, fishing, swimming, bicycling

 breakfast, dinner, Sun. brunch (dinner weekends off-season) wine & liquor available

 smoking discouraged

Woods Hole-Martha's Vineyard ferry (res. needed for car). In Edgartown, take first R. off Main St. to Summer St., continue ½ block to inn.

508-627-4751
South Summer St., Edgartown, MA 02539
Gery and Paula Conover, Innkeepers

Colonel Ebenezer Crafts Inn

This is a restored 1786 Colonial farmhouse on spacious landscaped grounds with a beautiful brick patio and swimming pool. Light and airy rooms, furnished with antiques and good reproductions, include a sunporch and a library filled with books. Quiet and peaceful, this gracious inn offers grand New England views, with the lively Publick House and its great food nearby.

 6 rooms, $98/$108 B&B
2 suites, $125/$135 B&B
Visa, MC, Amex

 all private baths

 open year-round

children accepted
no pets

swimming pool, golf, fishing, Sturbridge Village

 breakfast; dinner at Publick House, MAP available sherry available

 smoking allowed

conference facilities (22)

Hartford, I-84, Exit 2 to Sturbridge. Bear R. to stop sign & Publick House on L. From Mass. Tpke. Exit 9 to Exit 3B-Sturbridge Rte. 20 (1st exit) to Publick House on Rte. 131.

508-347-3313
% Publick House, Box 187, Sturbridge, MA 01566
Buddy Adler, Innkeeper

Hawthorne Inn

On land where Emerson, Alcott, and Hawthorne lived, and among trees planted by these illustrious men, the Hawthorne Inn follows their lead in the cultivation of art and appreciation of the spiritual in life. Friendly, caring innkeepers and nature walks, where land, sky, and water refresh the senses, imbue this winsome, intimate inn with a very special feeling.

 7 rooms, $85/$150 B&B
no credit cards

 all private baths

 open year-round

 children welcome
no pets

swimming (Walden Pond), museums, wooded trails for hiking & xc skiing, canoeing on Concord River

 breakfast

 smoking restricted

Rte. 128-95, Exit 30-B (W) (Rte. 2A) for 2.8 mi. Bear R. at fork toward Concord for 1.2 mi. Inn across from Hawthorne's home.

508-369-5610
462 Lexington Rd., Concord, MA 01742
Gregory Burch & Marilyn Mudry, Innkeepers

The Inn at Stockbridge

Consummate hospitality and outstanding breakfasts distinguish a visit at this turn-of-the-century Georgian Colonial estate on 12 secluded acres in the heart of the Berkshires. Close to Tanglewood, theaters, museums, and skiing, the inn has a gracious, English country house feeling, with two well-appointed living rooms, a formal dining room, and a baby grand piano.

 7 rooms, $75/$165 B&B
Visa, MC, Amex

 all private baths

 closed 2 wks. in March

children over 12
no pets

swimming pool, golf, tennis, hiking, skiing

breakfast; dinners for groups can be arranged complimentary wine

 smoking allowed

conference facilities (20)

Mass. Tpke. Exit 2 & (W) on Rte. 102 to Rte. 7 (N) 1.2 mi. to inn on R. From NYC, Taconic Pkwy. to Rte. 23 (E) & Rte. 7 (N) past Stockbridge 1.2 mi.

413-298-3337
Rte. 7 (North), Box 618, Stockbridge, MA 01262
Lee & Don Weitz, Innkeepers

Jared Coffin House

Early 19th-century buildings and one 18th-century house, all thoughtfully restored and decorated comprise this inn, conveniently located in Nantucket's Old Historic District, near Main Street shops and with easy access to island beaches and bike paths. The Tap Room and Jared's offer both casual and more formal dining.

 60 rooms, $50/$175 EP
Visa, MC, Amex, Diners

 all private baths

 open year-round

 children accepted
permission required for pets

 beaches, tennis, sailing,
biking

 all meals available
on premises
wine & liquor available

no pipes, cigars in restaurant

conference facilities (24)

Flights available from NYC, Boston, New Bedford, & Hyannis. Or take Hyannis ferry, leaving car in Hyannis — cars unnecessary on Nantucket.

508-228-2400; reservations: 508-228-2405 (M-F, 10-6)
29 Broad St., Nantucket, MA 02554
Philip & Margaret Read, Innkeepers

The Lenox Hotel

This small hotel has been run by the same family for over 25 years. In the Back Bay area, next to Copley Square, the hotel offers several rooms with working fireplaces and many with country-inn touches. Diamond Jim's Piano Bar and the Pub and Grill are popular attractions with guests and local residents alike. Valet parking service.

 219 rooms, $125/$210 EP
3 suites, $350 EP

 all private baths

 open year-round

 children accepted
no pets

all Boston attractions, health club, racquet ball, jogging paths

restaurant & room
service
wine & liquor available

wheelchair access (18 rooms)
conference facilities (200)

Mass Tpke., Exit 22, Copley Square ramp to L. on Dartmouth 2 blocks to L. on Newbury St. 1 block to L. on Exeter 1 block to hotel at corner of Exeter & Boylston.

800-225-7676; in Mass.: 617-536-5300
710 Boylston St., Boston, MA 02116
The Saunders Family, Innkeepers

Longfellow's Wayside Inn

Known as Howe's Tavern in 1716, the inn was immortalized in 1863 by Longfellow in his *Tales of a Wayside Inn*. Nothing could be more classic than this red clapboard, with white trim, sitting on a winding country road. A living museum filled with history and priceless antiques, it continues its mission to provide "ampler hospitality." Make reservations for rooms or dining far in advance.

 10 rooms, $56/$60 EP
Visa, MC, Amex, Diners

 all private baths

 closed Dec. 24 & 25

 children accepted
no pets

 historic sites, famous
Revolutionary War landmarks

 all meals
wine & liquor available

non-smoking dining area

Between Boston & Worcester off Rte. 20: 11 mi. (W) of Rte. 128 & 7 mi. (E) of Rte. 495. Sign on R. for Wayside Inn Rd.

508-443-8846
Wayside Inn Rd., off Rte. 20, South Sudbury, MA 01776
Francis Koppeis, Innkeeper

The Queen Anne Inn

Spacious guest rooms, antiques, garden views, private balconies, working fireplaces, and private whirlpool baths are a few of the amenities that may be found here on Cape Cod's picturesque south shore. The intimate restaurant features superb cuisine, and pursuits to beguile quiet hours or to engage the energetic are all around.

 29 rooms, $99/$179 B&B
1 suite, $199 B&B
Visa, MC, Amex, Diners

 all private baths; 2 Jacuzzis

 closed Dec. 1 thru April 15

 children accepted
kennel nearby for pets

indoor spa, 3 tennis courts, bikes, boating, scuba diving, fishing, golf

continental breakfast, dinner, dining room closed Tues.; 12/1—5/17 wine & liquor available

smoking discouraged

conference facilities (30)

Rte. 6 (E) to Exit 11, R. on Rte. 137 and L. on Rte. 28 for 3.5 mi. to light and R. fork to Queen Anne Rd. and up hill to inn.

508-945-0394; for reservations: 800-545-INNS
70 Queen Anne Rd., Chatham, MA 02633
Nicole & Guenther Weinkopf, Innkeepers

Ralph Waldo Emerson Inn

One of the last of the old summer hotels on Cape Ann, the Emerson's broad porches and Greek Revival architecture give it a classic majesty. Preserving the charm of yesteryear while keeping up with the times, the inn features a heated saltwater pool, a whirlpool and sauna, and a theater for movies. Popular seafood and shore specialties are always included on the menu.

 34 rooms, $72/$102 EP
2 suites, $81/$102 EP
Visa, MC, Discover

 all private baths

 closed Dec. 1 to Mar. 31

 children accepted
no pets

 saltwater pool, sauna, game room, VCR, golf, whale-watching, hiking, tennis

 breakfast & dinner, July—Labor Day; breakfast only April—July, Sept.—Nov.

 smoking accepted

 wheelchair access (2 rooms)
conference facilities (35)

Rte. 128 (N) to Rte. 127. At 1st light (L) on Rte. 127 (N). Follow to Pigeon Cove. Turn R. at inn sign on Phillips Ave.

508-546-6321
Phillips Ave., Box 2369, Rockport, MA 01966
Gary & Diane Wemyss, Innkeepers

The Red Lion Inn

This grand old inn in the Berkshire Hills is still the lively, delightful focus of village activity it has always been since 1773. Its broad, rambling porch, hung with summer pots of glowing fuchsias and festooned in winter with garlands and Christmas trees, welcomes travelers with cheerful cordiality, born of long tradition. Beautiful antiques and heirlooms abound.

 95 rooms, $44/$136 EP
10 suites, $106/$218 EP
Visa, MC, Amex, Discov.

 80 private baths; 4 shared baths

open year-round

children accepted
no pets

 exercise room, pool, golf, tennis, Tanglewood, Jacob's Pillow, Berkshire Theater Festival, Norman Rockwell Museum

 breakfast, lunch, & dinner
MAP available for groups
wine & liquor available

 non-smoking area in dining room

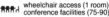 wheelchair access (1 room)
conference facilities (75-90)

I-90, Exit 2 at Lee, to Rte. 102 (W) to Stockbridge.

413-298-5545
Main St., Stockbridge, MA 01262
Jack & Jane Fitzpatrick, Owners; Betsy Holtzinger, Innkeeper

The Village Inn

In the center of the Berkshire village of Lenox, this Colonial inn, built in 1771, is close to shops, galleries, parks, beautiful wooded trails, Tanglewood, summer dance and theater festivals, winter skiing, fall foliage, and spring flower excursions. Country antiques, some 4-posters, fireplaces, fine American regional cuisine, and afternoon English tea will brighten your stay in the Berkshires.

 29 rooms, $40/$130 EP
Visa, MC, Amex, Diners

 27 private baths, 1 shared, 1 Jacuzzi

open year-round

 children over 6
no pets

 downhill & xc skiing, golf, riding, tennis, swimming, fishing

breakfast, English tea, dinner exc. Mon.

 non-smoking dining area

wheelchair access (3 rooms)
conference facilities (25)

Mass. Tpke. (I-90), Exit 2, Rte. 20(W) to Rte. 183(S). Turn L. for 1 mi. to R. on Church St. & inn. From Rte. 7 to Rte. 7A & Church St. in Lenox.

413-637-0020
16 Church St., P.O. Box 1810, Lenox, MA 01240
Cliff Rudisill & Ray Wilson, Innkeepers

The Weathervane Inn

This 200-year-old inn, listed on the National Register of Historic Places, is a small cluster of buildings set off the highway in a lovely little Berkshire village. All of today's amenities, including a swimming pool, along with many original architectural features enhance the warm, comfortable atmosphere. The food is wonderful.

 10 rooms, $90/$140 MAP
Visa, MC, Amex

all private baths

open year-round

 children over 7
no pets

 pool, nature walks, antiques, museums, tennis, golf, skiing, Tanglewood, summer theater

breakfast & dinner
B&B rates available
wine & liquor available

 no cigars or pipes

wheelchair access (2 rooms)
conference facilities (25)

 From NYC, Taconic Pkwy. to Rte. 23 (E) 13 mi. to inn on R. From Mass. Tpke., Exit 2 & Rte. 102 to Rte. 7 (S) to Rte. 23 (W) to inn on L.

413-528-9580
Rte. 23, South Egremont, MA 01258
Vincent & Anne Murphy, Innkeepers

MASSACHUSETTS

Yankee Clipper Inn

Fresh ocean breezes and sweeping panoramic views have greeted guests here for over 40 years. The Inn and the 1840 Bulfinch House, both with antique furnishings, and the more contemporary Quarterdeck all offer country inn blandishments. The cuisine is new New England, ocean-view dining is by candlelight, and life can be lazy or exciting, with fascinating Rockport close by.

22 rooms, $149/$203 MAP
5 suites, $185/$203 MAP
Visa, MC, Amex, Discov.

all private baths

closed Christmas Day

children over 3
no pets

swimming pool, tennis, golf,
whale-watching, deep sea fishing

breakfast & dinner
BYOB

no smoking in dining room

conference facilities (40)

Rte. 128 (N) to Cape Ann thru Gloucester. L. on Rte. 127 for 4 mi. to Rockport's 5 Corners & sharp L. & Pigeon Cove sign. Continue .5 mi. to inn.

508-546-3407
96 Granite St., P.O. Box 2399, Rockport, MA 01966
Bob & Barbara Ellis, Innkeepers

What Is A Country Inn?

When Norman Simpson first began writing about country inns, he was often asked to explain the term, and at first his answer would be, "a country inn is an inn in the country." Although all country inns were not then (or now) in the country, he felt that the word "country" was still operative. He said, "country implies an escape from urban pressures and demands, and not only conjures up euphoric bucolia but a welcome innocence associated with the American past. In many ways country inns are personified by some 19th-century attitudes concerning reliability, sincerity, warmheartedness, and a genuine desire to be of service. Each inn is original and unique, reflecting not only the old-time American ideal of rugged individualism, but also the personalities and tastes of the innkeeper-owners, who are more than likely on hand to make their guests feel personally welcome, comfortable, and at ease."

Although there were a number of specifics Norman looked for in an inn, his "bottom line" was always the people who ran it. One of his favorite expressions in referring to country inns was "personal hospitality," meaning the strong feeling of involvement and commitment on the part of the innkeeper, and a hospitable friendliness that came out of a genuine liking for people.

Among his personal set of requirements, beyond cleanliness, good housekeeping, maintenance, attractive furnishings with individuality, excellent service, and good food, were the little indications that the comfort and needs of the guests were being met: adequate lighting and an extra pillow for reading in bed, interesting reading material in guest rooms, generous-sized, thick towels, adequate shelf space in the bathroom, and all the special and personal touches, such as plantings, fresh flowers, music, paintings and artwork, and various and sundry articles of interest, that create the feeling of a "home away from home." He approved of the quiet afforded by the absence of television and telephones in guest rooms. He expected an inn to have at least one hospitable parlor or sitting room where guests could meet and talk in a convivial atmosphere.

He had a strong conviction that anything of a business or commercial nature should be kept to a bare minimum, and above all, the real thing, as opposed to the ersatz, should be used in furnishings as well as foods. If reproductions of antique furniture were used, they should be excellent reproductions, and if, God forbid, anything plastic was discovered, it had better be virtually invisible and of superior quality. Food should be fresh and made from scratch.

He felt that country inns should reflect their regions, and he was particularly happy when he found an inn that was rooted in its community with all the local color and flavor of the area.

A convivial place to meet new people, to have good conversation, to make friends, to relax or to be active—ultimately, to feel "at home." For Norman Simpson, these were the attributes of a good country inn.

Botsford Inn, Farmington Hills   4
Montague Inn, Saginaw   2
National House Inn, Marshall   3
Stafford's Bay View Inn, Petoskey   1

Botsford Inn

Restored by Henry Ford in the 1920s, with many of his personal furnishings still intact, this inn was originally built in 1836 and later became a stagecoach stop. Spacious grounds, a rose garden, and towering trees invite the many birds seen through the floor-to-ceiling windows of the restaurant, where a hearty menu is offered. Victorian-style village shops are nearby.

65 rooms, $55/$75 B&B
6 suites, $100/$150 B&B
Visa, MC, Amex, Diners

all private baths

closed Dec. 25 & Jan. 1

children welcome
no pets

garden courtyard, tennis courts, Kensington Park, YMCA, golf, xc & downhill skiing

breakfast daily; lunch & dinner served Tues.—Sun.
wine & liquor available

non-smoking dining areas

wheelchair access (2 rooms)
conference facilities (125)

I-94 (W) to I-275 (N). Exit M-102 & continue to Grand River & 8-Mile Rd. Inn is on L. with long picket fence.

313-474-4800
28000 Grand River Ave., Farmington Hills, MI 48024
John Anhut, Innkeeper

Montague Inn

Surrounded by 8 acres of spacious lawns, flower gardens, and trees beside a lake, this Georgian mansion, recently restored to its original splendor, provides a peaceful and elegant oasis in the heart of the city. Fine cuisine is offered in the intimate dining room overlooking the beautiful grounds.

18 rooms, $50/$130 B&B
Visa, MC, Amex

16 private baths; 1 shared bath

closed Christmas Eve/Day, New Year's

children accepted
no pets

library, lawn games, garden pool, tennis, antiquing

breakfast
lunch & dinner Tues. to Sat.
wine & liquor available

no smoking in guest rooms

wheelchair access (3 rooms)
conference facilities (40)

From I-75 exit on Holland Ave. (W) for 3.5 mi. Turn L. on Washington Ave., continue (S) 2 blocks to inn.

517-752-3939
1581 So. Washington Ave., Saginaw, MI 48601
Meg Brodie-Ideker, Innkeeper

The National House Inn

The town of Marshall, called the Williamsburg of the Midwest, has many citations for its 19th-century architecture, including the National Register of Historic Places, on which this inn is also listed. Michigan's oldest operating inn and the first brick building in the county, its restoration and renewal as a warm, hospitable inn, beautifully furnished, with lovely gardens, is a boon to all who visit here.

16 rooms, $68/$85 B&B
2 suites, $85/$92 B&B
Visa, MC, Amex

all private baths

closed Dec. 25

children welcome
no pets

gift shop, garden, park, tennis, antiquing, xc-skiing

breakfast & catered dinners

conference facilities (36)

I-94 to Exit 110; Rte. 27 (S) 2 mi. to Michigan Ave. Turn R. Marshall is halfway between Detroit & Chicago

616-781-7374
102 So. Parkview, Marshall, MI 49068
Barbara Bradley, Innkeeper

MICHIGAN

Stafford's Bay View Inn

Judged one of the "10 Best Inns" in the nation, this grande dame of classic Victorian architecture on Little Traverse Bay in the Historic Landmark Victorian cottage community of Bay View, sets the standard in fine dining and gracious service. Guests swim, sail the Great Lakes, rock on the front porch, cross-country ski out the front door, or enjoy the finest Alpine skiing in the Midwest.

 24 rooms, $50/$122 B&B
6 suites, $116/$160 B&B
Visa, MC, Amex

 all private baths

 open year-round

children welcome
no pets; kennel nearby

R hiking, xc skiing, beach, golf, tennis, boating, scenic drives

 breakfast, lunch, Sun. brunch
dinner on a seasonal basis

smoking allowed

wheelchair access (1 room)
conference facilities (60)

From Detroit, I-75 (N) to Gaylord exit, Rte. 32 (W) to Rte. 131 (N) Petoskey. From Chicago, I-94 to Rte. 196 (N) to Rte. 131 (N) to Petoskey.

616-347-2771
613 Woodland Ave., P.O. Box 3, Petoskey, MI 49770
Stafford & Janice Smith, Judy Honor, Innkeepers

Birth Of A Book

The story of how Country Inns and Back Roads *happened and how Norman became the recognized authority on country inns has been told many times in countless articles and reviews—his travels in the 1950s and '60s throughout New England for his advertising agency business, his boredom with stays in sterile motel and hotel rooms "staring at a television set," the discovery of off-the-beaten path inns where he felt at home and was able to relax and talk with the innkeepers and other guests, and finally, how, in 1966, writing as "The Berkshire Traveller," he put together, with his wife Nancy, a little 16-page booklet containing descriptions of 12 New England inns; called simply* Country Inns.

Having gotten a rather nice response to his first attempt, he wrote another book, and then another—this time adding "Back Roads" to the title, albeit in lower case. With each subsequent edition, which at first was issued twice a year and cost one dollar for a year's subscription, the number of inns and pages grew rather slowly. As he explained it, there weren't very many country inns around for him to write about. By the spring of 1969, the book had 40 pages with 28 inns in 10 states; the fall edition boasted 74 pages with 55 inns in 16 states. Norman had dipped down into the South and reached the Pacific Ocean.

By 1972, when the New York Times ran a 2-page article about Norman and his book, its popularity was unquestionable. He expanded his travels in the late 1970s to Europe and Britain and Ireland, and two more Country Inns and Back Roads books were born. Along with his travels and writing, he managed to continue publishing a few other books every year through his small publishing house, the Berkshire Traveller Press.

However, as he contemplated cutting back on his publishing business and concentrating on the IIA and his writing and traveling, he began to give serious consideration to offers to buy the Berkshire Traveller Press. In 1984 he received an offer from Harper & Row for Country Inns and Back Roads. The arrangements seemed ideal. Although Harper & Row would own the titles, Norman would retain complete control over all elements of the books and Harper & Row would print and market them. This arrangement continued until Norman's death in 1988. The 1989 editions of Country Inns and Back Roads—both North America and Europe—are the last of these books to be produced by Norman's company, the Berkshire Traveller Press.

The IIA has taken this opportunity to present its own publication, The Innkeepers' Register, to acquaint the public with the Association, its goals, and its fine country inn members.

The Berkshire Traveller Press, under new ownership, was commissioned to publish this book, thus preserving a valued and longstanding relationship.

St. James Hotel, Red Wing 2
Schumacher's New Prague Hotel, New Prague 1

St. James Hotel

Since 1875 a lodestone for travelers to the scenic Mississippi River city of Red Wing, nestled between limestone bluffs, this small, bustling hotel has been elegantly restored and outfitted. Impressive period furnishings, beautifuly crafted quilts, genuine hospitality, and such special touches as complimentary champagne and turn-down service are a few of the pleasures you'll find here.

60 rooms, $79/$115 EP
Visa, MC, Amex, Discov

all private baths (6 Jacuzzis)

open year-round

children accepted
no pets

shopping, antiquing, golf,
downhill & xc skiing, river boat
cruise

breakfast, lunch, dinner
Sun. brunch
wine & liquor available

7 non-smoking guest rooms

conference facilities

From Mpls./St. Paul, Hwy. 5 (E) exit Hwy. 55, across Mendota Bridge 25 mi. to U.S. Hwy. 61 in Hastings. Hwy. 61 (S) 25 mi. to Red Wing & Main & Bush Sts.

612-388-2846
406 Main St., Red Wing, MN 55066
Gene Foster, General Manager

Schumacher's New Prague Hotel

Schumacher's New Prague Hotel is a charming Central-European inn, internationally known for its superb Czech and German cuisine by Chef/Proprietor John Schumacher. Bavarian folk-painted furniture, eiderdown comforters, whirlpool tubs for two, and gas fireplaces transport you to Middle Europe. Intimate Bavarian bar and Central-European Gift Shop add to the uniqueness of this inn.

11 rooms, $70/$138 EP
Visa, MC, Amex, Discov

all private baths, 8 Jacuzzis

closed Dec. 24, 25

no children
no pets

18-hole golf course, xc skiing,
biking, fishing

breakfast, lunch, dinner
wine, beer, & liquor available

no pipes or cigars

conference facilities (11)

From Mpls., 35W (S) to Exit 3B Shakopee (Hwy. 13) (S) for 4 mi. L. on Hwy. 13 (S) for 28 mi. to R. on Hwy. 19 (W). Continue past center of New Prague to inn.

612-758-2133
212 W. Main St., New Prague, MN 56071
Kathleen & John Schumacher, Innkeepers

Covers of three of the little booklets published by Norman Simpson in 1966-67.

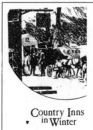

NEW HAMPSHIRE

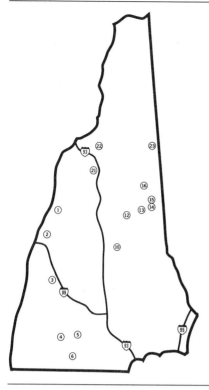

Birchwood Inn, Temple 6
Christmas Farm Inn, Jackson 16
Corner House Inn, Center Sandwich 12
Darby Field Inn, Conway 15
Dexter's Inn and Tennis Club, Sunapee 3
Hickory Stick Farm, Laconia 10
Inn at Crotched Mountain, Francestown 5
John Hancock Inn, Hancock 4
Lovett's by Lafayette Brook, Franconia 21
Lyme Inn, Lyme 1
Moose Mountain Lodge, Etna 2
Philbrook Farm Inn, Shelburne 23
Rockhouse Mountain Farm Inn, Eaton Center 14
Spalding Inn & Club, Whitefield 22
Stafford's in the Field, Chocorua 13

Birchwood Inn

Rufus Porter murals grace the small candlelit dining room of this family-run, original inn, resting by the common of a quiet Colonial town. On the National Register of Historic Places, the inn features guest and common rooms filled with interesting antiques and country dining with fresh foods prepared to order and carefully presented by the innkeepers.

7 rooms, $55/$70 B&B
personal checks accepted

breakfast; dinner Tues.—Sat.
BYOB

private & shared baths

no pipes or cigars

closed 2 wks. in April;
1 wk in Nov.

children over 10
no pets

Temple is on Rte. 45, 1.5 mi. (S) of
Rte. 101, 10 min. (E) of Peterborough.

hiking, antiquing, skiing,
golf, swimming

603-878-3285
Route 45, Box 197, Temple, NH 03084
Judy & Bill Wolfe, Innkeepers

Christmas Farm Inn

In a setting of majestic mountains, crystal-clear rivers, and leafy woods, the cluster of buildings that make up this rambling inn invite the visitor to share the good life. Whether inside in cozily decorated rooms, outside at the garden swimming pool, or in the candlelit dining room feasting on delectable, freshly-made meals, guests enjoy the at-home feeling.

20 rooms, $136/$156 MAP
10 suites, $150/$164 MAP
Visa, MC, Amex

breakfast & dinner
wine & liquor available

all private baths, 2 Jacuzzis

non-smoking main dining room

open year-round

conference facilities (50)

children accepted
no pets

From Rte. 16 to Rte. 16A, across
covered bridge .5 mi. to school-
house. R. on Rte. 16B for .5 mi. to
inn on R.

swimming pool, putting green,
game room, shuffleboard, xc &
downhill skiing, golf, tennis

603-383-4313
Box CC, Route 16B, Jackson, NH 03846
Sydna & Bill Zeliff, Innkeepers

Corner House Inn

The picturesque village of Center Sandwich and the surrounding area, with "Golden Pond" (Squam Lake) and mountain trails, offer delightful diversions in any season. And a warm welcome awaits at the intimate 100-year-old Corner House, sparkling with country-Victorian antiques and beautiful crafts made by many local artisans and craftspeople. Food is special and fresh.

 4 rooms, $60/$70 B&B
Visa, MC, Amex

 1 private, 1 shared bath

 closed Thanksgiving, Dec. 25, part of Nov. & April

 children over 4
well-behaved pets allowed

 crafts & antiques shops, museum, art gallery, Squam Lake, tennis, hiking, skiing

 breakfast, lunch, & dinner
wine & liquor available

smoking discouraged

conference facilities (70)

I-93, Exit 23 & Rte. 104 (E) to Meredith. R. at light onto Rte. 25 (E) to Center Harbor. L. at 2nd light to Bean Rd. for 7 mi. to yellow blinker. R. onto Main St. to inn.

603-284-6219
Main St., P.O. Box 204, Center Sandwich, NH 03227
Jane & Don Brown, Innkeepers

The Darby Field Inn

Beguiling guests with a spectacular view of distant mountains from its dining room, many guest rooms, and terrace swimming pool, this 1830 inn on the edge of the White Mountain National Forest is a favorite with outdoor enthusiasts. Well-groomed ski and hiking trails past rivers and waterfalls, a cozy pub, a massive stone fireplace, and hearty, delicious food are part of the picture.

 15 rooms, $82/$160 MAP
1 suite, $122/$180 MAP
Visa, MC, Amex

 14 private, 1 shared baths

 closed Mar. 19 thru Apr. 27; Oct. 22 thru Nov. 21

 children accepted
no pets

 swimming pool, xc ski trails, canoeing, golf, tennis, hiking, rock climbing

 breakfast & dinner
wine & liquor available

smoking restricted

Rte. 16 (N) toward Conway. Turn L. .5 mi. before Conway at inn sign, 1 mi. to 2nd inn sign. Turn R. & continue 1 mi. to inn.

800-426-4147 or 603-447-2181
P.O. Box D, Bald Hill, Conway, NH 03818
Marc & Marily Donaldson, Innkeepers

Dexter's Inn & Tennis Club

Tennis buffs love Dexter's, but so do all the guests who come for the breathtaking views, idyllic gardens, green lawns, bright guest rooms, and excellent, bountiful food. The Simpson-Durfor family runs the inn like a well-appointed private home, offering friendly service and advice on the myriad diversions available in the area.

 17 rooms, $115/$155 MAP
1 cottage, $350 MAP
Visa, MC

 all private baths

 closed Nov. 1 to May 1

 children accepted
pets accepted

 3 tennis courts, pool, lawn games, lake activities, hiking, golf

 breakfast, dinner; lunch also in July/Aug.
wine & liquor available

smoking accepted

wheelchair access (1 room)
conference facilities (25)

I-89 (N), Exit 12 & Rte. 11 (W) for 8 mi. to L. on Winn Hill Rd. for 1.5 mi. From I-91 (N), Exit 8 & Rte. 11/103 (E) for 18 mi. to Newport & Rte. 103 for .1 mi. to L. on Young Hill Rd. for 1.2 mi.

800-232-5571 or 603-763-5571
Box R, Stagecoach Rd., Sunapee, NH 03782
Michael Durfor & Holly Simpson-Durfor, Innkeepers

Hickory Stick Farm

Since 1950 the Roeder family has been serving thoughtful meals in the delightful Early American atmosphere of their converted Colonial farm buildings. Two charming B&B guest rooms have been added as well as a screened gazebo with splendid mountain view. The trip over winding roads through quiet woods is part of the fun.

 2 rooms, $60 B&B
Visa, MC, Amex, Diners, CB

 all private baths

 closed Mon.; restaurant closed Oct. 12 to May 30

 children over 7
no pets

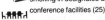 hiking, nature trails, birdwatching, swimming, boating, skiing, Shaker Village

 breakfast (guests only) & dinner
wine & liquor available

smoking in designated areas

conference facilities (25)

I-93, Exit 20 & Rte. 3 toward Laconia, approx. 5 mi. over Lake Winnisquam bridge .3 mi. to R. on Union Rd. for 1.5 mi. & sharp R. Around bend to L. on Bean Hill Rd. for .5 mi. to inn.

603-524-3333
Rte. 2, Box 398, Laconia, NH 03246
Scott Roeder, Innkeeper

The Inn at Crotched Mountain

An awe-inspiring setting and a spectacular view of Piscataquog Valley makes all the difference at this out-of-the-way Colonial inn. Walking and ski trails thread the woods; vegetable and flower gardens supply food and adornment for tables and rooms. Rose Perry's savory home cooking has the added zest of an occasional Indonesian dish.

 13 rooms, $60/$120 MAP
no credit cards

 private & shared baths

 closed end of ski season to mid-May; late Oct. to Thanksgiving

 children accepted
pets accepted

 swimming pool, tennis courts, xc and walking trails, downhill skiing, antique shops, summer theaters

 breakfast, dinner; wine & liquor available

 cigars or pipes restricted

wheelchair access (4 rooms)
conference facilities (26)

From Manchester, Rte. 101 (W) to 114 (N) to Goffstown & 13 (S) to New Boston & 136 (W) to Francestown. R. at 47 (N) 2.5 mi. to L. on Mountain Rd. for 1 mi. to inn.

603-588-6840
Mountain Rd., Francestown, NH 03043
Rose & John Perry, Innkeepers

The John Hancock Inn

This inn opened its doors 200 years ago and has been the center of activity in this lovely Colonial village (National Register of Historic Places) ever since. Reminders of a kinder, gentler day abound, including c. 1824 Rufus Porter murals and Moses Eaton stencils. Warm hospitality, quiet country comforts, and creative, traditional meals welcome guests.

 10 rooms, $65/$75 EP
Visa, MC

 all private baths

 closed 10 days early spring & late fall; Dec. 24 & 25

 children accepted
pets accepted

historic touring, walking, antiquing summer theater, year-round sports

 breakfast, lunch, dinner, Sun. brunch
wine & liquor available

conference facilities (35)

From Keene, Rte. 9 (N) to Rte. 123 (E) to Hancock. From Peterborough, Rte. 202 (N) & L. on Rte. 123 to Hancock.

603-525-3318
Main St., Hancock, NH 03449
Glynn & Pat Wells, Innkeepers

Lovett's Inn by Lafayette Brook

In a peaceful woodland setting at the northern edge of Franconia Notch State Park, this c. 1784 central chimney Cape Cod (National Register of Historic Places) is in the heart of ski country—both downhill and cross-country. Choices among guest rooms include fireplaces, mountain views, color TV, and air conditioning; all are attractive and comfortable. Food is hearty and delicious.

 30 rooms, $85/$162 MAP
Visa, MC, Amex, Diners

 private & shared baths

 closed April to mid-May
Nov. to mid-Dec.

 children accepted
no pets

xc skiing, pool, golf, hiking, tennis, horseback riding

breakfast & dinner
EP available
wine & liquor available

non-smoking dining area

wheelchair access (several rooms)
conference facilities (50)

On I-93N, Exit 3 (Franconia Notch Pkwy.) L. onto Rte. 18 (N), 3 mi. to inn on L. On I-91 (N), exit 17 (Wells River, VT). Rte. 302 (E) to Rte. 117 (E). R. on Rte. 18 (S), 2 mi. inn on R.

603-823-7761; (outside N.H.) 800-356-3802
Profile Rd., Route 18, Franconia, NH 03580
Lan Finlay, General Manager

The Lyme Inn

A treasure-trove of New England memorabilia and antiques, with braided rugs, a fascinating collection of samplers and other folk art, and an engaging old-world atmosphere, the Lyme Inn is not far from Dartmouth College. Master chef Hans Eickert offers an interesting mix of continental and New England cuisine, and innkeepers Fred and Judy Siemons tender warm New England hospitality.

 12 rooms, $96/$136 MAP
2 suites, $130/$150 MAP
Visa, MC

 12 private, 1 shared baths

 closed Thanksgiving to late Dec.; Apr. 1—21

 children over 7
no pets

Dartmouth College, skiing, swimming, golf, tennis, canoeing

breakfast & dinner
wine & liquor available

no cigars in dining room

I-91, Exit 14. Follow signs for Lyme. Inn is in center of town on the common.

603-795-2222
On the Common, Lyme, NH 03768
Fred & Judy Siemons, Innkeepers

Moose Mountain Lodge

Perched high on the side of Moose Mountain, with hiking and ski trails threading through 350 acres of woods and meadows, this big, old, comfortable lodge enjoys wonderful everchanging views of the Connecticut River Valley. Meals are healthy, plentiful, and delicious, beds are restful, and the welcome is warm and friendly. Far from the sounds of civilization, peace and quiet reigns supreme.

 12 rooms, $90 B&B/$150 AP
Visa, MC

5 shared baths

closed Mar. 21 to May 31;
Nov. 1 to Dec. 26

children over 5
no pets

 hiking & skiing trails, swimming pond, large porch, Appalachian Trail, Connecticut River

 breakfast, lunch & dinner in winter; breakfast & dinner, summer & fall

no smoking

I-89, Exit 18 (N) to Rte. 120 for .5 mi. to R. at Etna Rd. for 3.6 mi. to R. on Rudsboro Rd. for 2 mi. to L. on Dana Rd. for .4 mi. up mtn. to lodge.

603-643-3529
Moose Mountain Rd., P.O. Box 272, Etna, NH 03750
Peter & Kay Shumway, Innkeepers

Philbrook Farm Inn

The latchstring has been out at this venerable (National Register of Historic Places) New Hampshire inn since 1861, and 5 generations of the Philbrook family have been dispensing New England hospitality and wholesome, hearty, home-cooked New England meals ever since. As they say, "you will find simplicity rather than luxury, genuineness rather than pretension" at this peaceful retreat.

 19 rooms, $80/$100 MAP
2 cottages in summer
no credit cards

private & shared baths

closed April 1 to May 1;
Nov. 1 to Dec. 25

children welcome
pets accepted in cottages

 swimming pool, game room, stable, major ski areas, nat'l. forest hiking

 breakfast, lunch, dinner
B&B rates available
BYOB

 wheelchair access (3 rooms)

U.S. Rte. 2, (W) from Bethel, ME, or (E) from Gorham, NH. At inn sign turn on Meadow Rd. for 1 mi. to R. at North Rd. for .5 mi. to inn.

603-466-3831
North Rd., Shelburne, NH 03581
The Philbrook & Leger Families, Innkeepers

Rockhouse Mountain Farm Inn

This picturesque and informal inn is tucked away on the side of a mountain, amidst 400 acres of forests, streams, fields, and wildflowers. There are farm animals for children, horses for riding, ponds and a lake for swimming and boating, and hearty scrumptious meals, with fresh vegetables from the garden and fresh-baked breads and desserts.

 15 rooms, $92/$104 MAP
3 bunk rooms, $32 p.p. MAP
no credit cards

private & shared baths

closed Nov. 1 to June 15

children welcome
no pets

 shuffleboard, riding, fields & woods, 3 ponds, swimming, boating, hiking trails, tennis, golf

 breakfast & dinner
BYOB

smoking accepted

 wheelchair access (2 rooms)
conference facilities (40)

I-93, Exit 23 & Rte. 104 (E) to Meredith & Rte. 25 (N) to Rte. 16 (N) to Conway and Rte. 153 (S) to Eaton Center.

603-447-2880
Eaton Center, NH 03832
The Edge Family, Innkeepers

Spalding Inn & Club

Understated, discreet elegance marks the decor and atmosphere of this resort-inn, where championship lawn bowling tournaments are held. Tennis courts, a swimming pool, and a 9-hole golf course take up part of the 400 acres of lawns, gardens, and orchards. The tea room and lounge feature live piano music, and the dining room features attentive service and delicious food.

 54 rooms, $180/$220 AP
16 suites, $210/$350 AP
Visa, MC, Amex, Diners

all private baths

closed mid-Oct to mid-June

children accepted
pets with prior approval

 pool, tennis, lawn bowling, putting green, par 3 golf course, shuffle-board, nearby golf, summer theater, fishing, hiking

 breakfast, lunch, dinner
MAP available
wine & liquor available

smoking allowed

 wheelchair access (18 rooms)
conference facilities (125)

I-93 (N) to Littleton exit to Rte. 116 thru Whitefield to Mtn. View Rd. intersection—3 mi. north of village.

603-837-2572
Mountain View Rd., Whitefield, NH 03598
William A. Ingram & Lore Moran, Innkeepers

Staffords-in-the-Field

This circa 1778 Federalist country house inn is coming into its 25th season. In a rural setting, surrounded by open fields and forest with walking trails, the inn's herb garden flavors the scrumptious gourmet meals served in the Lantern Lite dining room. Guest rooms are furnished with country antiques and down quilts, and there's a wonderful large porch for just sitting and viewing.

 12 rooms, $120/$180 MAP
4 cottages, $120/$180 MAP
Visa, MC, Amex

 9 private, 3 shared baths

 open year-round

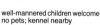 well-mannered children welcome
no pets; kennel nearby

walking trails, tennis, croquet, xc skiing, golf, swimming, climbing, antiques

 breakfast & dinner
wine & liquor

 no smoking in dining room

wheelchair access (2 rooms)

From Chocorua Village & Rte. 16, take Rte. 113 (W) for 1 mi. to inn sign. From Rte. 93, Exit 23 to Rtes. 104 & 25 (E) to Rte. 16 (N) to village & Rte. 113 as above.

603-323-7766 or 800-332-0355
Box 270, Chocorua, NH 03817
The Stafford Family, Innkeepers

Who Are The Innkeepers?

Innkeepers who can lay claim to being the third or fourth generation of an innkeeping family are a rare breed, indeed. They have had the advantage of growing up in an inn and becoming thoroughly conversant and comfortable with the intricacies of innkeeping. There are only a very few of these younger innkeepers who are able to draw on a wealth of past experience.

Since the mid-1970s, more and more people have followed the dream of owning a lovely country inn, enjoying a slower-paced lifestyle and the opportunity to be creative and independent far away from urban pressures and the "fast track."

This dream has brought into the world of innkeeping such diverse types as advertising executives, investment bankers, school teachers, airline stewardesses, management consultants, engineers, interior decorators, social workers, architects, political speech writers, and many others who have left successful careers.

Some innkeepers came out of training in large hotel chains; many are graduates of hotel management schools and culinary institutes. A few are master chefs.

As is so often the case, the reality does not live up to the dream in all respects. Innkeeping is a hard taskmaster—the hours are long, the demands on time, energy, patience, perseverance, humor, and cash are great. However, the rewards, too, are great. There is the pride of accomplishment in creating an independent way of life, and in seeing the results of hard work, ingenuity, and creativity paying off.

Beyond the satisfaction of operating a successful inn is the sense of the personal pleasure in knowing that guests truly enjoy themselves and appreciate the atmosphere of the inn.

Innkeepers sometimes develop longstanding friendships with guests who return for visits over many years. In fact, just as there are a few third- and fourth-generation innkeepers, so there are a few third- and fourth-generation guests. This is more likely to happen at resort-type inns, where families spend their vacations year after year.

Innkeepers or their assistants have many kinds of personal interactions with guests, sometimes sharing a recipe for a particularly favored dish, tracking down a baby sitter or the location of some esoteric antiques dealer, finding lost eyeglasses, mapping out a scenic drive, verifying a quotation in a book, recommending a doctor, a mechanic, a jeweler, or. . . . Making reservations at restaurants, reserving tickets for concerts and the theater, and calling taxis are among the more usual services in metropolitan areas.

This is just a glimpse at the kind of dedicated, intelligent, and friendly people who are keepers of country inns.

Garden State Parkway

Inn at Millrace Pond, Hope   1
Mainstay Inn & Cottage, Cape May   3
Stockton Inn, "Colligans," Stockton   2

Garden State Parkway

The Inn at Millrace Pond

The 1769 gristmill in the historic village of Hope has been converted into a lovely inn, with additional rooms in the Millrace House and the stone Wheelwright's Cottage. In a green and peaceful setting along Beaver Brook, this authentically restored and furnished Colonial inn, offers a seasonal American menu and gracious service in the tradition of Colonial hospitality.

 16 rooms, $65/$95 B&B
Visa, MC, Amex

breakfast; Sun. brunch;
dinner, Tues. thru Sun.
wine & liquor available

all private baths

 open year-round

wheelchair access (1 room)
conference facilities (65)

children accepted (limited)
no pets

antiquing, hiking, canoeing,
skiing, golf, winery tour

From I-80, Exit 12, take Rte. 521 (S)
1 mi. to blinker, L. on Rte. 519 (N),
.2 mi. to inn. From the south, Rte.
78 to Rte. 519 (N), travel 18 mi. take
R. at blinker .2 mi. to inn.

201-459-4884
Rte. 519, P.O. Box 359, Hope, NJ 07844
Dick Gooding & Gloria Carrigan, Innkeepers

The Mainstay Inn

Once an exclusive gentlemen's gambling club, the Mainstay is now an elegant Victorian inn furnished in splendid antiques. Breakfast and afternoon tea are served each day either in the formal dining room or on the wide veranda. Located in Cape May's famous historic district, the inn is within walking distance of beaches, interesting shops, and a vast selection of fine restaurants.

 10 rooms, $80/$115 B&B
 2 suites, $85/$125 B&B
no credit cards

breakfast, afternoon tea

all private baths

 closed mid-Dec. to mid-March

no smoking

 conference facilities (24)

children over 12 accepted
no pets

croquet, swimming, tennis,
golf, biking, birdwatching

Take Garden State Pkwy. (S). In
Cape May, Pkwy. becomes Lafayette
St. Take L. at first light onto
Madison Ave. Go 3 blocks, R. at
Columbia Ave. Inn on R.

609-884-8690
635 Columbia Ave., Cape May, NJ 08204
Tom and Sue Carroll, Innkeepers

The Stockton Inn, "Colligan's"

Serving travelers since 1796, with a colorful history and many colorful, famous guests, this inn is probably most known for having inspired the Rodgers and Hart song, "There's a Small Hotel With a Wishing Well." Two fine restaurants, contemporary American and classical French, complement the beautiful suites, gardens, and fireplace-warmed dining rooms.

 3 rooms, $60/$95 B&B
 8 suites, $80/$130 B&B
Visa, MC, Amex, Diners

lunch, dinner, Sun. brunch
wine, liquor & beer available

all private baths

 closed Dec. 25

pipes & cigars restricted

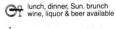 conference facilities (60)

no children
no pets

canoeing, rafting, tubing,
ballooning, fishing

N.J. Rte. 29 (River Rd.) 3 mi. (N) to
Stockton. Inn is in center of town
on Main St. (Across the river from
New Hope, PA)

609-397-1250
Main St., P.O. Box C, Stockton, NJ 08559
Andrew McDermott, Innkeeper

NEW MEXICO

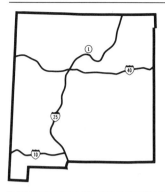

Grant Corner Inn, Santa Fe   1

Grant Corner Inn

505-983-6678
122 Grant Ave., Santa Fe, NM 87501
Louise Stewart & Pat Walter, Innkeepers

This elegant and delightful inn has an ideal location just two blocks from the historic plaza of downtown Santa Fe, among intriguing shops, galleries, and restaurants. Lush gardens, beautifully appointed guest rooms, fabulous gourmet breakfasts, and the gracious hospitality of the Walters family make this an experience not to be missed. Ample parking on the premises.

 13 rooms, $45/$110 B&B
Visa, MC

 private & shared baths

 closed Jan.

children over 6
no pets

skiing, hiking, fishing,
golf, tennis, swimming (fee)

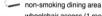 complimentary breakfast;
picnic lunches, catered dinners
complimentary wine

non-smoking dining area

wheelchair access (1 room)
conference facilities (20)

From Albuquerque, I-25 (N) Exit St. Francis L. (N) 3 mi. to R. at Alameda (W) .6 mi., L. (N) on Guadalupe .1 mi., R. (W) on Johnson .1 mi., parking on L.

Where Might A Country Inn Be Found?

In restored villages and historic districts, where the ambience of the past is celebrated and preserved . . .

In the heart of farm country, surrounded by fields and meadows . . .

On lakes, deep in the woods, where the cry of a loon or the sigh of wind through the trees are the loudest sounds to be heard . . .

On river fronts, with views of barges and boats plying the waterways . . .

On ranches in the western desert, surrounded by magnificent mountain ranges, where the influence of the native Indians and early Spanish settlers is still felt . . .

On quiet village streets lined with trees or beside village greens . . .

On tiny islands off both the Atlantic and the Pacific coasts, with dunes, sea grasses, sandy beaches, marine life, and vast ocean views . . .

In college towns and near summer camps . . .

On back roads, among rolling hills, in mountain fastnesses, beside rushing streams and gurgling brooks . . .

In busy small towns, where the history of our country had its earliest beginnings . . .

In former Shaker and Moravian settlements and Amish communities . . .

Near state parks and forests and nature preserves . . .

In West Coast towns, amid masses of flowers, close to the sea, in the mountains, in wine country, or right in the heart of the big city . . .

On former estates with hundreds of acres of meadows, hills, and woods, and often with animals for watching and petting . . .

Asa Ransom House

Asa Ransom built his original log home and tavern on this spot in 1801, and the tradition of old-fashioned hospitality lives on in this antique-filled, lovingly decorated inn. The food is second to none, with herbs and fresh vegetables from the garden, fresh-baked, whole-grain breads, and delicious homemade ice creams, like raspberry chocolate chip. Non-smoking dining rooms.

 4 rooms, $75/$95 B&B
Visa, MC, Discov

 all private baths

 closed Fri. & Sat. weekly;
month of Jan.

 well-supervised children welcome
no pets

 Niagara Falls, many antique
shops within walking distance

 breakfast for houseguests
dinner Sun. thru Thurs.
wine & liquor available

 no smoking

Traveling (E): I-90, Exit 49, L. on Rte. 78 for 1 mi. to R. on Rte. 5 for 5.3 mi. Traveling (W): I-90, Exit 48A & R. on Rte. 77 for 1 mi. to R. on Rte. 5 for 10 mi. to inn.

716-759-2315
10529 Main St. (Rte. 5), Clarence, NY 14031
Bob & Judy Lenz, Innkeepers

The Bark Eater

On a spacious farm nestled in the heart of the Adirondacks, this homey and informal inn is a haven, offering simple but gracious accommodations, memorable dining, and many opportunities to savor the great outdoors. Originally a 19th-century stagecoach stop between Lake Champlain and Lake Placid, the inn continues its 150-year-old tradition of hospitality.

 17 rooms, $110 B&B
Amex

 4 private, 4 shared baths

 open year-round

 children accepted
no pets

 horseback riding, swimming,
hiking, fishing, all summer &
winter sports

 breakfast, trail lunch,
dinner

 smoking restricted

 wheelchair access (4 rooms)
conference facilities (34)

From Keene: Rte. 73 (W) 1 mi. to R. at Alstead Hill Rd. for .5 mi. up hill.

518-576-2221
Alstead Hill Rd., Box 139, Keene, NY 12942
Joe-Pete Wilson, Innkeeper

Beekman Arms

The focus of activity in busy, bustling, historic Rhinebeck, this inn has seen much history being made since 1766 when its original section was built. Today, in addition to its authentically furnished Colonial Tap Room and guest rooms, there are many attractive, recently built rooms with working fireplaces, and a beautiful greenhouse dining area where casual but elegant country fare is served.

 54 rooms, $60/$95 EP
2 suites, $95/$125 EP
Visa, Amex, Diners

 all private baths

 open year-round

 children accepted
no pets in Delamater House

 Hyde Park, Rhinebeck WWI
Aerdrome, Culinary Instit. of Amer.,
golf, tennis, xc skiing

breakfast, lunch, dinner
wine & liquor available

non-smoking dining area

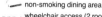 wheelchair access (2 rooms)
conference facilities (25)

NY Thruwy. (I-90) Rhinecliff Bridge Exit to Rte. 9 (S) 2 mi. to Rhinebeck Village. From Taconic Pkwy. take Rte. 199 (W) to L. on Rte. 308 to Rhinebeck Village.

914-876-7077
4 Mill St., Route 9, Rhinebeck, NY 12572
Chuck La Forge, Innkeeper

Benn Conger Inn

Reflecting the personal interests of the innkeepers, this inn offers fine food, an extensive wine cellar, and a comfortable but not precious atmosphere. It is filled with good books, jazz records, and beautiful prints. This is a stately Greek Revival mansion on 18 acres of rolling land, great for cross-country skiing and nature walks.

 1 room, $60 B&B
3 suites, $70/$100 B&B
Visa, MC, Amex, Diners

 all private baths

 closed March

 children over 10 accepted
no pets

 hiking, xc skiing, library, golf,
tennis, antiques, shopping

breakfast, houseguests
dinner, houseguests and public
wine & liquor available

smoking limited

From I-81, Exit 12 (Homer), (S) on Rte. 281 for 3 mi., take R. (W) on Rte. 222 for 10 mi. to Groton, crossing Rte. 38, making no turns. Inn, up the hill, on R.

607-898-5817
206 West Cortland St, Groton, NY 13073
Mark and Pat Bloom, Innkeepers

The Bird & Bottle Inn

A famed landmark on the old Albany-New York post road since 1761, this inn continues to welcome travelers with traditional Hudson River Valley hospitality. An authentic old country inn, it is internationally renowned for its gourmet cuisine and comfortable, cozy rooms with woodburning fireplaces, 4-poster or canopied beds, and Colonial furnishings.

 2 rooms, $185 MAP
2 suites, $205 MAP
Visa, MC, Amex, Diners

 all private baths

 closed Jan. 1—20

 children not accepted
pets not accepted

 hiking, nature walks, golf,
xc skiing, boating

breakfast, dinner, Sun. brunch
wine & liquor available

smoking accepted

 conference facilities (50)

From Rte. I-84 Fishkill: (S) 8 mi. on Rte. 9. Inn on L. From NYC and Westchester: (N) on Rte. 9A and 9, past Croton and Peekskill. Inn 8 mi. beyond Peekskill on Rte. 9 in Garrison area.

914-424-3000
Old Albany Post Rd. (Rte. 9), Garrison, NY 10524
Ira Boyar, Innkeeper

Garnet Hill Lodge

The Log House of this rustic resort-inn was built in 1936, and the big fireplace in the living/dining room of varnished pine is a place where guests gather for conversation and fun. Nestled in the Adirondacks overlooking 13th Lake, amid spectacular scenery, the inn features hearty meals for hungry guests after a day of bracing outdoor activity.

 21 rooms, $110/$150 MAP
no credit cards

 all private baths

 closed Nov. 15—30

 children accepted
no pets

 swimming, tennis, hiking,
boating, fishing, xc skiing,
museums, downhill skiing

breakfast, lunch, dinner
wine & liquor available

non-smoking dining area

 conference facilities (60)

From Albany, on I-87 exit 23 (Warrensburg). (N) on Rte. 9 to Rte. 28. (N) on Rte. 28, 22 mi. to North River. L. on 13th Lake Rd., 4.5 mi. to inn.

518-251-2821
13th Lake Rd., North River, NY 12856
George and Mary Heim, Innkeepers

The Genesee Country Inn

This 1833 stone mill in beautiful Genesee country has been converted into a charming inn on 6 unique acres of woods, spring-fed millponds, and waterfalls. Guest rooms are charmingly decorated with authentic stenciling, some oversized canopied beds, fireplaces, and wooded views. Breakfast and afternoon tea is served in common rooms, and there are gardens and outside decks.

 9 rooms, $80/$115 B&B
Visa, MC, Amex, Diners

 all private baths

 open year-round

 no pets

 trout fishing, walking, biking, Genesee Country museum-village nearby. Color TV, A/C

 breakfast, houseguests luncheon for conferences BYOB

wheelchair access (1 room)
conference facilities (14)

From NY Thruway (I-90) take Exit 47 and Rte. 19 S. to LeRoy. Go (E) on Rte. 5 to Caledonia, (N) on Rte. 36 to Mumford. L. on George St.

716-538-2500
948 George St., Box 340, Mumford, NY 14511
Glenda and Gregory Barcklow, Innkeepers

Greenville Arms

The former country mansion of William Vanderbilt now welcomes guests into an environment filled with reminders of its gracious Victorian past. Surrounded by 7 beautifully landscaped acres, with a swimming pool, the inn's atmosphere is homey and inviting, with wonderful old-fashioned country meals. The natural beauty of the Catskill Mountains is close at hand.

 19 rooms, $110/$150 MAP
$70/$110 B&B
Visa, MC, Amex

 private and shared baths

 open year-round

 children accepted
no pets

 breakfast, dinner

 non-smoking dining room

conference facilities (20)

 swimming pool, lawn games, hiking, tennis, golf, glider rides

Exit N.Y. Thruway at 21B. Turn L. on 9-W, (S) 2 mi. to traffic light. R. on 81(W), 13 mi. to Greenville. L. at traffic light onto 32S. Inn on the right.

518-966-5219
South St., Greenville, NY 12083
Laura and Barbara Stevens, Innkeepers

The Holloway House

This family-run restaurant is in a beautiful Federal-style building, which began life as a stagecoach stop in 1808. For the last 30 years the Wayne family has been serving sumptuous homestyle food to ever-returning appreciative guests. Their roast turkey dinner, Sally Lunn bread, orange rolls, and pies are famous. East Bloomfield is a historically fascinating area.

 restaurant, no rooms
Visa, MC, Amex

 closed end of Nov.
to early April

 children accepted
no pets

 Sonnenberg Gardens, golf, communications museum, Finger Lakes, race track

 lunch, dinner
closed Mon.
wine & liquor available

smoking & non-smoking areas

wheelchair access (in back)

From NY Thruway, Exit 45, L. onto 96 (S). 3 mi. to Victor. R. at third traffic light. Maple Ave. (S) 5 mi. to Holcomb. R. at light, 2 blocks. L. to Rtes. 5 & 20.

716-657-7120
Rtes. 5 & 20 East Bloomfield, NY 14443
The Wayne Family, Innkeepers

Lincklaen House

Built in 1835 as a luxurious stopover for Colonial travelers, the Lincklaen House has long been a local landmark and has hosted such luminaries as President Grover Cleveland and John D. Rockefeller. The old-world atmosphere is now combined with modern comfort and gracious service, offering guests a return to an era of elegant hospitality.

 18 rooms, $65/$95 B&B
3 suites, $100/$130 B&B
Visa, MC, Amex

 all private baths

 open year-round

 children accepted
pets accepted

swimming, golf, tennis

 lunch, dinner daily
breakfast Sat. & Sun.
wine & liquor available

smoking accepted

conference facilities (75)

From NY Thruwy. (I-90). Exit 34, take Rte. 13 (S) to Cazenovia. R. on Rte. 20, 1 block. From I-81: Exit 15 (La Fayette), E. on Rte. 20. 18 miles to Cazenovia.

315-655-3461
79 Albany St., Box 36, Cazenovia, NY 13035
Howard M, Kaler, Innkeeper

Mill House Inn

Transformed from a working sawmill into a country inn with Central European architecture and ambience, the inn's guest rooms all have an individual feeling, with fireplace suites for the romantic at heart. The rock gardens, shaded paths, and brook all have a peaceful and soothing effect, within a short distance of all the attractions of the Berkshires.

 7 rooms, $75/$85 B&B
4 suites, $90/$135 B&B
Visa, MC, Amex

all private baths

closed Mar. 15—May 15
Nov. 1—Dec. 15

children accepted (limited)
no pets

swimming pool, golf, tennis,
bicycling, skiing

continental breakfast

no smoking

wheelchair access (1 room)

From NYC, Taconic Pkwy. (N), Exit Rte. 295, R. to Rte. 22. L. to Rte. 43, R. for 1.2 mi. to inn. From Boston, Mass. Tpke. (I-90), Exit B3, Rte. 22 (N) to Rte. 43.

518-733-5606
Rt. 43, Stephentown, NY 12168
Frank and Ronnie Tallet, Innkeepers

Oliver Loud's Inn

Feeding the ducks, building a snowman, visiting nearby shops, or rocking on the porch overlooking the Erie, are some ways to relax at this 174-year-old stage-coach inn. Stunningly and authentically furnished with antiques and period art-work, the inn pampers its guests with a split of champagne and homemade cookies, as well as a breakfast hamper delivered to your room.

 8 rooms, $125 B&B
Visa, MC, Amex, CB

all private baths

open year-round

children over 12 welcome
no pets; kennel nearby

Erie Canal towpath for hiking, jogging, xc skiing, biking, boating, golf, tennis, major museums, and many sightseeing opportunities

 breakfast baskets, snacks
Richardson's Canal House restaurant
wine & liquor available

 smoking/non-smoking rooms

wheelchair access (1 room)
conference facilities (20)

NY Thruway (I-90) Exit 45, to I-490 (W) for 3 mi. to Bushnell's Basin exit, turn R. & continue to Marsh Rd. signal & bear R. to inn.

716-248-5200
1474 Marsh Rd., Pittsford, NY 14534
Vivienne Tellier, Innkeeper

The Redcoat's Return

Peg and Tom Wright's easy cordiality has been making guests comfortable for 17 years, and Tom's English accent and his artistry in the kitchen (he was a chef on the Queen Mary) keeps them coming back for more. Whether it's snuggling up in front of a roaring fire, hiking, or enjoying spectacular views of the Catskills, it's always fun at this romantic, cozy inn.

 14 rooms, $75/$100 B&B
Visa, MC, Amex, Diners

private & shared baths

closed Apr. to Memorial Day wkend
closed Nov. —reopen Thanksgiving

call for acceptance
no pets

downhill & xc skiing, golf, tennis, swimming, boating, horseback riding

 breakfast, dinner
wine & liquor available

 pipes & cigars restricted

N.Y. Thruway (N), Exit 20 (Saugerties). L. to Rte. 32 (N). Rte. 32 merges with Rte. 32A and at light, with 23A (W). At next light, L. onto County Rd. 16, 4.5 mi. to R. on Dale Lane. Inn on R.

518-589-6379
Dale Lane, Elka Park, NY 12427
Tom and Peggy Wright, Innkeepers

Rose Inn

This 1851 Italianate mansion is a gem of woodcraft, with a stunning circular staircase of priceless Honduran mahogany. The high-ceilinged rooms are furnished with antiques from around the world, and the inn is surrounded by 20 landscaped acres. Cornell University, Finger Lakes wineries, dozens of antique shops, and Cayuga Lake are nearby. Member of Romantik Hotels.

 12 rooms, $85/$125 B&B
3 suites, $150/$200 B&B
Visa, MC, Amex

all private baths

open year-round

children over 10 accepted
no pets; kennel next door

all lake sports, skiing, tennis, golf, wineries, Cornell University

 breakfast
dinner prix fixe by reservation
wine available

no smoking

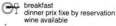 conference facilities (20)

From Ithaca, Rte. 13 (N), Exit Rte. 34 (N), 6 mi. to "T" (red flashing light). R. for .5 mi. to fork, stay L. Inn is 3.2 mi. on R.

607-533-7905
Rte. 34 North, P.O. Box 6576, Ithaca, NY 14851-6576
Charles and Sherry Rosemann, Innkeepers

The Sedgwick Inn

This historic country inn, once a stagecoach stop, sits on 12 acres in the Berkshire's beautiful Taconic Valley. Colonial, with Victorian overtones, the inn's rooms are handsomely furnished in antiques and interesting artifacts, including the original 1791 indentures. Gourmet dinners are served in the Coach Room Tavern.

 4 rooms, $70/$75 B&B
 1 suite $90 B&B
Visa, MC, Amex, Diners

 all private baths

 open year-round

 children accepted in annex
pets accepted in annex

 library, gift and gourmet shops, downhill & xc skiing, swimming, theatre, Tanglewood Music Festival, Art Museums

 breakfast, dinner
wine & liquor available

no smoking in guest rooms

wheelchair access in annex
conference facilities (60)

From Albany: Rte. 787 (N) to Troy. Exit Rte. 2 (E) to Rte. 22. R. on Rte. 22 (S), 6 mi. to inn. From N.Y.C.: Taconic Pkwy (N), Exit Rte. 295 (E) to Rte. 22. L. on Rte. 22 (N) for 22 mi.

518-658-2334
Rte. 22, Box 250, Berlin, NY 12022
Bob and Edie Evans, Innkeepers

The Sherwood Inn

From the handsome lobby with its fireplace and baby grand piano to the pleasant guest rooms, many of which overlook beautiful Skaneateles Lake, gracious service and comfort are the keynotes here. American cuisine with a Continental touch is served in several dining rooms and the friendly, casual tavern. The lovely village of Skaneateles is interesting and offers many activities.

 11 rooms, $66/$83 B&B
 5 suites, $94/$99 B&B
Visa, MC, Amex, Diners, CB

 all private baths

 open year-round

 children accepted
pets accepted

swimming, boating, golf, downhill and xc skiing, fishing, bicycling, hiking

 breakfast, lunch, dinner
dining room closed 12/24 & 25
wine & liquor available

non-smoking dining area

conference facilities (100)

From N.Y. Thruway: Exit Weedsport, Rte. 34 (S) to Auburn. (E) on Rte. 20, 7 mi. to Skaneateles. From (S): Rte. 8 (N) to Cortland, Rte. 41 (N) to Skaneateles. L. on Rte. 20, for 1 mi.

315-685-3405
26 West Genesee St., Skaneateles, NY 13152
William Eberhardt, Owner; Ellen Seymour, Innkeeper

Springside Inn

Perhaps "inn of flowers" would be a good name for this 1830 red clapboard building, with its masses of flowers in gardens, tubs, baskets, and window boxes. On 8 acres of lawns and trees, with a spring-fed pond and ducks, this homey, comfortable chef-owned inn offers delicious food along with dinner theater in the summer.

 9 rooms, $55 B&B
Visa, MC, Amex

 private and shared baths

 closed Memorial Day, July 4, Dec. 25

 children accepted
no pets

summer dinner theatre, hiking, swimming, boating, fishing, xc skiing, tennis, winery tours

 continental breakfast, dinner
 Sun. brunch
wine & liquor available

no smoking in guest rooms

conference facilities (310)

From N.Y. Thruway: Exit 40, take Rte. 34 (S) thru Auburn to Rte. 38 (S) to traffic circle at lake. Take 2nd exit R. at (W) shore of Owasco Lake. .25 mi. to inn.

315-252-7247
41-43 West Lake Rd., Auburn, NY 13021
The Dove Family, Innkeepers

The White Inn

The White Inn is an impressive c. 1868 edifice with a pillared portico, beyond which are beautifully restored and decorated rooms. Superb cuisine has gained an enthusiastic following among guests and townsfolk. The famous Chautauqua Institution, not far, has varied cultural programs; there is sailing on Lake Erie in the inn's boat, and there are summer concerts in the town's Victorian bandstand.

 11 rooms, $45/$80 B&B
9 rooms, $70/$130 B&B
Visa, MC, Amex

 all private baths

open year-round

children accepted
no pets

bicycling, wineries, antiquing, skiing, SUNY college activities, Chautauqua Institution

 breakfast, lunch, dinner
wine & liquor available

non-smoking dining area

wheelchair access (3 rooms)
conference facilities (60)

NY Thruwy, Exit 59. At traffic light. L. on Rte. 60 (S) to traffic light, R. on Rte. 20 (W), Main St. Inn on R.

716-672-2103
52 East Main St., Fredonia, NY 14063
David Palmer and David Bryant, Innkeepers

William Seward Inn

Formerly the home of Lincoln's secretary of state and a New York governor, this 1821 Greek Revival mansion overlooks the eastern rim of Lake Erie. Puffy comforters adorn antique 4-posters in lovely guest rooms; sumptuous breakfasts are served in the cheery dining room. Wineries, a national antiques center, Chautauqua Institution, and downhill and cross-country skiing are nearby.

10 rooms, $58/$84 B&B
Visa, MC

all private baths

open year-round

children over 12 accepted
no pets

hiking, Chautauqua touring, fishing, golf, sailing, downhill and x-country skiing

breakfast; Sat. dinner available by res. in Jan./Feb.

no smoking

conference facilities (23)

From N.Y. Thruwy (I-90), Exit 60. L. onto Rte. 394 (E) (Portage Rd.) thru Westfield. Inn on right 4 mi. from toll booth

716-326-4151
R.D. 2 South Portage Rd. (Rte. 394), Westfield, NY 14787
Peter and Joyce Wood, Innkeepers

Matters Of Some Moment

Significant to the architectural heritage of our country, to communities, and to the public in general, is the reclamation of many historic and beautiful old buildings that have been brought back to life as country inns. Many of them are now listed on the National Register of Historic Places.

It was a slow process at first but, as interest in country inns grew, many wonderful things began to happen. For example, some of the inns of the 18th and 19th centuries that had been converted to other uses came back into their own. False ceilings were ripped away to find beautiful, heavy beams. Walls were removed to disclose handsome fireplaces. Layers of wallpaper were carefully peeled away to reveal beautiful 18th-century stenciling. Several inns in New England were discovered to have on their walls in remarkably preserved condition, the works of the famous itinerant artists, Rufus Porter and Moses Eaton. Porter was known for his murals and Eaton for his stencils. `

Other valuable materials which have been (and are still being) saved and preserved are carved marble mantelpieces, beautiful glazed tiles, pressed tin ceilings, stained-glass windows, intricately carved moldings and balustrades, and various kinds of inlaid woods. Numerous previously lost or forgotten arts and crafts of construction and interior decoration have been recovered in the process.

Many buildings were saved from being torn down literally in the nick of time. In addition to the reclamation of former inns, buildings of all descriptions and former uses have been pressed into service. Former mansions and private residences are the most frequent beneficiaries of these conversions, but country inns may be found today in structures which were originally used as gristmills, barns, riding stables, log cabins, poorhouses, boarding houses, hospitals, schools, private clubs, and mountain lodges, to name a few.

Perhaps best of all, many American communties without village inns or small hotels since the late Victorian days find a new vigor and pride in their own restored inns and historic buildings, and the public is able to appreciate our architectural heritage and is enriched by having these beautiful old buildings available and accessible.

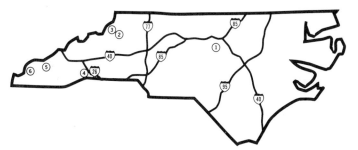

Fearrington House, Chapel Hill   1
Hemlock Inn, Bryson City   5
Hound Ears Lodge,
   Blowing Rock   2
Mast Farm Inn, Valle Crucis   3
Orchard Inn, Saluda   4
Snowbird Mountain Lodge,
   Robbinsville   6

The Fearrington House

In a cluster of low, attractive buildings grouped around a courtyard and surrounded by gardens and rolling countryside, this elegant inn offers luxurious quarters in a country setting. A member of Relais et Chateaux, the restaurant's sophisticated regional cuisine, prepared in the classical techniques, has received national acclaim.

5 rooms, $95/$125 B&B
9 suites, $135/$175 B&B
Visa, MC, personal checks

all private baths

closed Dec. 24-26

no children
no pets

swimming, biking, walking, bird-watching, golf, tennis, sailing, fishing

breakfast, lunch, dinner
Tues. thru Sun.
wine; BYOB

smoking limited

wheelchair access (1 room)
conference facilities (40)

Chapel Hill, U.S. 15-501 (S) 8 mi. to village of Fearrington.

919-542-2121
Fearrington Village Center, Pittsboro, NC 27312
Jenny & R.B. Fitch, Owners

Hemlock Inn

High, cool, quiet, and restful, this inn is beautifully situated on top of a small mountain on the edge of the Great Smoky Mountains National Park. There's a friendly informality in the family atmosphere and authentic country furniture. Honest-to-goodness home-cooking and farm-fresh vegetables are served bountifully from Lazy Susan tables.

23 rooms, $91/$110 MAP
3 cottages, $91/$124 MAP
no credit cards

all private baths

closed mid-Nov. to mid-April

children welcome
no pets

hiking, ping-pong, shuffleboard, skittles, Smoky Mtn. NatL. Park, tubing, Cherokee Indian Res.

breakfast at 8:30 A.M.;
dinner at 6 P.M., Mon. to Sat.
& 12:30 P.M. Sun.

non-smoking dining room

wheelchair access (8 rooms)

Hwy. 74, Hyatt Creek Rd.-Ela exit & bear R. to L. turn on Hwy. 19 for approx. 1 mi. to R. turn at inn sign. Take country road 1 mi. to L. turn at next inn sign.

704-488-2885
Galbreath Creek Rd., P.O. Drawer EE,
Bryson City, NC 28713
Ella Jo & John Shell, Innkeepers

Hound Ears Lodge

Families come to this Alpine-style resort in the Blue Ridge Mountains to golf, play tennis, ski, dine in the 4-star restaurant or relax and browse in local antiques shops. A centerpiece for its country club community, the elegant lodge, with its relaxing atmosphere and friendly staff, many of them college students, puts guests right at ease.

23 rooms, $170/$244 MAP
4 suites, $170/$268 MAP
Visa, MC, Amex

all private baths

closed March

children accepted
no pets; kennels nearby

golf, tennis, pool, skiing, weight room, sauna

all meals from
April 1 to Jan. 2
BYOB

smoking accepted

conference facilities (60)

Winston-Salem Hwy. 421 (W) to Boone. Turn L. on Hwy. 105 (S) approx. 7 mi. Look for inn sign. Hickory, NC, Hwy. 321 (N) to Boone; L. on Hwy. 105 (S) approx. 6 mi. Look for inn sign.

704-963-4321
P.O. Box 188, Blowing Rock, NC 28605
David Blust, Innkeeper

Mast Farm Inn

Whether it's relaxing before a cheery winter fire or rocking on the wraparound front porch enjoying the summer view of the mountain valley, life at this newly restored, antique-filled inn (National Register of Historic Places) is pleasant and peaceful. Rooms are simple, clean, and cozy and the food is country cooking with a gourmet touch.

10 rooms, $70/$105 MAP
2-room house, $110/$124 MAP
Visa, MC

9 private, 1 shared baths

closed Mar. 6 to April 25;
Nov. 6 to Dec. 26

children over 12 accepted
no pets

fishing, hiking, skiing,
golf, canoeing

breakfast, houseguests only
dinner, Tues.-Sat.; Sun. lunch
BYOB

no smoking

wheelchair access (1 room)

Boone/Banner/Elk accessible from any direction. NC Rte. 105 (N) for 2.6 mi. Watch for Valle Crucis & Mast Farm sign.

704-963-5857
P.O. Box 704, Valle Crucis, NC 28691
Sibyl & Francis Pressly, Innkeepers

The Orchard Inn

A truly memorable dining experience is having a marvelous dinner to the strains of Mozart and Schumann on the glassed-in wraparound porch with its breathtaking view of the southern Blue Ridge Mountains. This turn-of-the-century country house has a touch of plantation elegance, with a large fireplace, many antiques, folk art, and masses of books and magazines to beguile guests.

9 rooms, $85/$100 B&B
3 cottages, $95/$115 B&B
no credit cards; personal checks

all private baths

open year-round

children over 12 accepted
no pets

walking paths, birding, antiquing,
Biltmore Estate, Blue Ridge
Parkwy, golf

breakfast, houseguest only
dinner by reservation
BYOB

no smoking

conference facilities (20)

I-26, NC Exit 28 & turn toward Saluda for 2 mi. to L. on Hwy. 176 for .5 mi. to inn on R.

704-749-5471
P.O. Box 725, Saluda, NC 28773
Ann & Ken Hough, Innkeepers

Snowbird Mountain Lodge

High up in Santeetlah Gap, not far from the giant hardwood trees of the Joyce Kilmer virgin forest, is this secluded, rustic, and picturesque mountain lodge, built of chestnut logs and native stone. Huge fireplaces, comfortable beds in pleasant rooms, a spectacular view, and plentiful, delicious meals make this an exceptional vacation retreat.

23 rooms, $98/$104 AP
Visa, MC, Amex

21 private, 1 shared baths

closed mid-Nov. to late April

children over 12 accepted
no pets

scenic hiking trails, game room,
ping-pong, billiards, shuffleboard,
horseshoes, stream fishing,
trout fishing, Joyce Kilmer forest

breakfast, lunch, dinner
BYOB

non-smoking dining room

wheelchair access (4 rooms)

Robbinsville, at Hardees, Rte. 129 (N) for 1.5 mi. to L. on NC Rte. 1116 for 3.3 mi. to R. at stop sign (Rte. 1127) for 6.7 mi. to lodge.

704-479-3433
275 Santeetlah Rd., Robbinsville, NC 28771
The Rhudy Family, Innkeepers

Rates are quoted for 2 people for 1 night and do not necessarily include service charges and state taxes. For more detailed information, ask the inns for their brochures.

AP — American Plan (3 meals included in room rate)

MAP — Modified American Plan (breakfast & dinner included in room rate)

EP — European Plan (meals not included in room rate)

B&B — Bed & Breakfast (breakfast included in room rate)

R — represents recreational facilities and diversions either on the premises of an inn or nearby

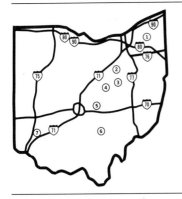

The Buxton Inn

Looking very much like a typical New England village, this college town bears the imprint of the pioneers who settled here in 1805. A short 7 years later the Buxton Inn began dispensing hospitality and sustenance and hasn't stopped yet. Noted nationally for its gourmet kitchens, with an intriguing mixture of antique furnishings and modern amenities, it continues its proud tradition.

 12 rooms, $65/$70 B&B
7 suites, $70/$85 B&B
Visa, MC, Amex

 all private baths

 closed Dec. 25, Jan. 1

 children accepted
no pets

 golf, tennis, swimming,
bicycling

 breakfast, lunch, dinner
Sat. and Sun. brunch
wine & liquor available

smoking accepted

 wheelchair access (2 rooms)
conference facilities (60)

From I-70: take Rte. 37 exit. (N) for 8 mi. on Rte. 37 into Granville. From Columbus: take Rte. 16 (E) for 25 mi. into Granville.

614-587-0001
313 E. Broadway, Granville, OH 43023
Orville and Audrey Orr, Innkeepers

The Golden Lamb

This illustrious inn (National Register of Historic Places) in America's heartland, the oldest in Ohio, has been in continuous operation since 1803, during which it has hosted 10 U.S presidents, Mark Twain, Charles Dickens, and Henry Clay. Antique-laden guest rooms boast the names of famous visitors, and everywhere are reminders of a lively and fascinating history. Exceptional cuisine.

 17 rooms, $55/$70 B&B
1 suite, $85 B&B
Visa, MC, Amex, Diners

all private baths

 dining room closed Dec. 25

children accepted
no pets

 golf, tennis nearby

 lunch & dinner, Mon.—Sat.
Sun.—Dinner only
wine & liquor available

non-smoking dining area

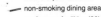 conference facilities (80)

From I-75 Exit at Rte. 63. Take Rte. 63 (E) 7 mi. to Lebanon. From I-71 Rte. 48 (N) 3 mi. to Lebanon. Inn at corner of Main (Rtes. 48 & 63) and Broadway.

513-932-5065
27 S. Broadway, Lebanon, OH 45036
Jackson Reynolds, Innkeeper

The Inn at Cedar Falls

The deceptively rustic 1840 Log House is an open-kitchen dining room, serving the most refined of gourmet dishes, prepared from home-grown produce. Guest rooms in the barn-shaped inn building combine antique beds, private baths, and sweeping views of meadows, woods, and wildlife. The rugged and beautiful Hocking Hills State Park flanks the inn on three sides.

 9 rooms, $51/$75 B&B
Visa, MC

all private baths

 open year-round

children's accommodations limited
no pets

 hiking, hammocks, swimming,
canoeing, riding

 breakfast; dinner by reservation
lunch for special occasions
BYOB

specified smoking areas

 wheelchair access (1 room)
conference facilities (18)

From Columbus: Rte. 33 (S) to Logan exit, R. on Rte. 664, 9.5 mi., L. on Rte. 374. Inn is 1 mi. on L.

614-385-7489
21190 State Route 374, Logan, OH 43138
Anne Castle, Innkeeper

OHIO

The Inn at Honey Run

Nestled in 60 acres of woods and pasture in the heart of Ohio's Amish country, this contemporary inn is both restful and invigorating—imbued with a spirit that seems to recharge its guests. The heartland cuisine features fresh trout, fruits, and vegetables. Many of the guest rooms in the main building and the earth-sheltered Honeycombs have woodburning fireplaces and patios.

 35 rooms, $50/$150 B&B
1 suite, $120 B&B
Visa, MC, Amex

breakfast, lunch, dinner
BYOB for guest rooms only

all private baths

no smoking in dining room

closed Jan. 2-15

conference facilities (72)

children accepted
no pets

birdwatching, nature trails, game room, Amish country, craft shops, cheese factories, golf, tennis

From Millersburg: Rtes. 62/39 (E) for 2 blocks. L. on Rte. 241 (N) for 1.9 mi. R. (E) on County Rd. 203 for 1.5 mi.

216-674-0011
6920 County Road 203, Millersburg, OH 44654
Marjorie Stock, Innkeeper

Welshfield Inn

A lively village hotel in the 1800s, this famous old landmark is now renowned as a wonderful country restaurant with real country cooking. Antiques, lace tablecloths, silver, fresh flowers, and costumed waitresses add a genteel and festive touch to the informal atmosphere. For 39 years owner/chef Brian Holmes has been turning out delectable meals for delightful guests from far and wide.

 restaurant, no rooms
Visa, MC, Amex

lunch & dinner
wine & liquor available

non-smoking dining room

closed Mons.; July 1—15; Fri. after Thanksgiving; Dec. 18—Feb. 1

conference facilities (50)

seeing-eye dogs only

Sea World

Ohio Tpke. (E) Exit 14 to U.S. 422 Welshfield for 20 mi. to inn, midway between Cleveland & Youngstown, (E) of Ohio 700.

216-834-4164
14001 Main-Market Rd., U.S. 422, Burton, OH 44021
Brian & Polly Holmes, Innkeepers

White Oak Inn

This turn-of-the-century home is a warm haven nestled in the middle of nowhere, with a spacious front porch for swinging or rocking, a common room with a fireplace, and guest rooms with antique furnishings and handmade quilts. Family-style cooking makes dining a memorable experience. The friendly atmosphere will refresh your spirit.

6 rooms, $70/$80 B&B
1 suite, $90 B&B
Visa, MC

breakfast, dinner
Sun. brunch

all private baths

no smoking

closed Easter, Thanksgiving, Christmas

conference facilities (20)

children over 12 accepted
no pets

lawn games, bicycling, Amish touring, antiquing, golf

From I-71: Rte. 36 (E) or Rtes. 95 (E) and 13 (S) to Mt. Vernon. Then U.S. Rte. 36 (E) 13 mi. to Rte. 715. From I-77: Rte. 36 (W) 43 mi., to Rte. 715. Take Rte. 715 (E) 3 mi. to inn.

614-599-6107
29683 Walhonding Rd. (S.R. 715), Danville, OH 43014
Joyce and Jim Acton, Innkeepers

The Wooster Inn

The spacious campus of the College of Wooster is the setting for this pleasant inn, which overlooks the college golf course, where inn guests may play. Tastefully decorated rooms offer modern comfort and quiet, and cuisine in the attractive dining room is excellent and fresh. The Ohio Light Opera and college events provide cultural and recreational diversions.

15 rooms, $59/$64 B&B
2 suites, $74/$98 B&B
Visa, MC, Amex, Diners

breakfast, lunch, dinner
wine & beer available

all private baths

closed Dec. 25

conference facilities (40)

children accepted
pets accepted

golf, tennis, Amish settlements, Football Hall of Fame in Canton. Wooster College activities

I-71 (S) to Burbank. L. on Rte. 83 (S), 18 mi., Wooster Exit, R. at Rte. 585 (S) for 200 ft. R. at Wayne Ave. Inn .7 mi. on L.

216-264-2341
801 E. Wayne Ave., Wooster, OH 44691
Willy J. Bergmann, Innkeeper

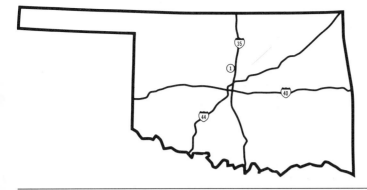

Harrison House, Guthrie   1

Harrison House

405-282-1000
124 W. Harrison, P.O. Box 1555, Guthrie, OK 43044
Phyllis Murray, Innkeeper

Here is a gem of Victoriana in a handsome red brick building in the center of historic and restored Guthrie, celebrating its centennial. Transformed from an impressive 1902 bank building into a charmingly decorated, beautifully appointed, and invitingly warm country inn, it perfectly expresses the pioneering spirit and character that typifies a gentler, bygone era.

 23 rooms, $40/$80 B&B
Visa, MC, Amex, Discov

 breakfast
wine available

 all private baths

smoking accepted

 open year-round

 conference facilities (100)

children accepted
no pets

From I-35: Exit 157 from (N); Exit 153 from (S). From (N): (W) 1.6 mi. on Noble to Division, L. 3 blocks to Harrison. R. 1 block. From (S): 4.3 mi. on Division to Harrison, L. 1 block.

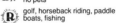 golf, horseback riding, paddle
boats, fishing

Guest Evaluations Are Encouraged

Members of the IIA are pledged to uphold standards of excellence in the maintenance and operation of their inns. Suggestions and comments from guests as to improvements are not only welcome, but actively encouraged. We are always happy to hear when we are doing something well, and positive feedback energizes and motivates us. However, sometimes we "can't see the forest for the trees," and guests, coming from an entirely different perspective, by giving us their suggestions, can help us correct matters that have escaped our attention.

Here is a possible check list that guests might follow in the evaluating an inn:

1) Were you greeted and served with a spirit of hospitality throughout your stay?

2) Was the guest room equipped with your comfort and safety in mind?

3) Does the inn evidence high standards of housekeeping and mainte-nance?

4) Was the food/service in the dining room/restaurant (or area restau-rants) of high quality?

5) Does the inn reflect an atmosphere and individuality that is consis-tent and appropriate?

6) Did you receive value for your dollar?

7) Would you return to this inn?

The IIA strongly encourages guests to send their comments and suggestions to the IIA office: Independent Innkeepers' Association, Stockbridge, MA 01262. Requests for information will be gladly received between 9 A.M. and 5 P.M. EST, Monday through Friday; 413-298-3636 or 800-344-5244.

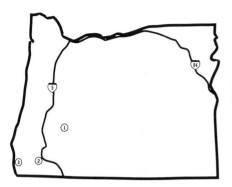

Paradise Ranch Inn, Grants Pass 2
Steamboat Inn, Steamboat 1
Tu Tu' Tun Lodge, Gold Beach 3

Paradise Ranch Inn

The natural beauty of Oregon envelops you here in green Rogue River Valley, and this friendly resort-inn has something for everyone. Mattie and Ollie have been running the ranch for 20 years, with help from others in the Raymond family, extending their special brand of hospitality to guests who love the magnificent views of lake and mountains.

 14 rooms, $55/$88 B&B
4 suites, $79/$125 B&B
Visa, MC

 all private baths, 2 Jacuzzis

closed Dec. 25

children accepted
no pets

 tennis, swimming, fishing, boating, white-water rafting, horseback riding, golf, volleyball, bicycling

 breakfast, lunch, dinner
wine & liquor available

 non-smoking areas

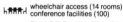 wheelchair access (14 rooms)
conference facilities (100)

From S.F. Rte. 101 (N) to Crescent City & Rte. 199 to Grants Pass & Rte. 5 (N) & exit at Merlin. Go under Rte. 5 & R. on Monument Dr. for 2.5 mi. to ranch on L.

503-479-4333
7000-I Monument Dr., Grants Pass, OR 97526
Ollie & Mattie Raymond, Innkeepers

Steamboat Inn

Imagine being lulled to sleep by sounds of the North Umpqua River! Nestled among towering firs, this inn's comfortable, cozy streamside cabins and hideaway cottages provide luxurious privacy. Gourmet meals served in a convivial atmosphere, the Umpqua National Forest with its hiking trails, waterfalls, and the river—a steelhead fisherman's dream—are just a taste of the delights here.

 8 cabins, $67, EP
5 cottages, $97, EP
Visa, MC

all private baths

limited services in winter

 children accepted
no pets

 fishing for steelhead, 35 mi. of public water, backpacking, hiking

breakfast, lunch
dinner by reservation
wine & beer available

 no smoking

 wheelchair access—inquire
conference facilities (50)

I-5 to Roseburg. Steamboat Inn is 38 mi. (E) on Rte. 138. Inn is 70 mi. (W) of Crater Lake and 40 mi. (W) of Diamond Lake, on Rte. 138.

503-496-3495 or 498-2411; FAX 498-2411 (2 rings + ★2)
Steamboat, OR 97447
Sharon and Jim Van Loan, Innkeepers;
Patricia Lee, Manager

Tu Tú Tun Lodge

"Casual elegance in the wilderness" is the key phrase at this civilized lodge, nestled between the forest and the Rogue River, not far from the rugged Oregon coast. Guests enjoy hors d'oeuvres around the large stone fireplace, congenial gourmet dining, and madrone wood fires on the terrace at dusk. Exciting boat trips, Chinook salmon fishing, or relaxing in solitude are options here.

 16 rooms, $90/$93 EP
2 suites, $120/$130 EP
Visa, MC

 all private baths

closed Oct. 31 to April 27

 children very welcome
pets welcome

 heated pool, player piano, 4-hole pitch & putt, horseshoes, pool table, salmon & steelhead fishing, hiking, white-water jet boat trips

breakfast, lunch, dinner
MAP available
wine & liquor available

 no smoking in dining room

 wheelchair access (8 rooms)
conference facilities (40)

Gold Beach, Hwy. 101 (E) 7 mi. along north side of Rogue River to lodge.

503-247-6664
96550 North Bank Rogue, Gold Beach, OR 97444
Dirk & Laurie Van Zante, Innkeepers

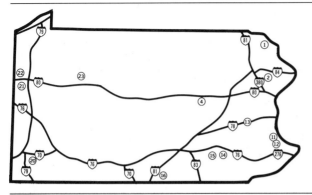

Barley Sheaf Farm

Barley Sheaf is an early Bucks County farm comfortably situated at the end of a long tree-lined drive. Once owned by playwright George S. Kaufman, Barley Sheaf fulfills everyone's expectations of what a romantic country inn should be. The hospitality is likewise everything one might hope for. Exceptional guest rooms, gracious common rooms and an outstanding breakfast.

 10 rooms, $100/$150 B&B
Amex

 all private baths
 closed Dec. 17 to Jan. 7

 children over 8
no pets

pool, historic touring, shopping, antiquing

breakfast

smoking allowed

 conference facilities (20)

On Rte. 202, .5 mi.(W) of Lahaska. From N.J. take Rte. 202. From Rte. 276 and south, take Rte. 263(N) to Buckingham and Rte. 202 to inn.

215-794-5104
Route 202, Box 10, Holicong, PA 18928
Ann & Don Mills, Innkeepers

Cameron Estate Inn

The Cameron Estate Inn and Restaurant occupy the rural Lancaster County estate of Simon Cameron, Abraham Lincoln's first Secretary of War. Rooms at Cameron are furnished in a grand style and are individually decorated; 7 have working fireplaces. The restaurant offers a fine selection of French food as well as the appropriate wines. Groff's Farm Restaurant, the county's finest, is also nearby.

 18 rooms, $60/$105 B&B
Visa, MC, Amex, Diners

 16 private, 1 shared baths
 open year-round

 children over 12
no pets

library, TV, lawn games, swimming, & tennis nearby

breakfast, lunch, dinner
Sun. brunch
wine & liquor available

smoking allowed

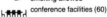 conference facilities (60)

Rte. 283 to Rte. 772(S) to 1st light in Mt. Joy and R. on Main to L. at next light (Angle St.) to R. on Donegal Springs Rd. for 4 mi. to the inn.

717-653-1773
R.D. 1, Box 305, Donegal Springs Rd., Mount Joy, PA 17552
Abram & Betty Groff, Innkeepers

Century Inn

It's not hard to believe this is the oldest operating inn (1794) on the National Pike (U.S. 40) when you see the hand-forged crane in the original kitchen and the vast array of rare antiques adorning this intriguing inn. Called one of the dining super stars in the Pittsburgh area, the inn is a favorite destination for both country inn buffs and gourmands.

 5 rooms, $65/$80 EP
 4 rooms, $90/$110 EP
no credit cards

 all private baths
 closed Dec. 23—Feb. 13

 children accepted
no pets

tennis, croquet,
many small shops in Scenery Hill

breakfast, houseguests only;
lunch, dinner
wine & liquor available

smoking accepted

 conference facilities (175)

From I-70, Bentleyville Exit. Rte. 917(S) to Rte. 40. 1 mi. (E) to the inn.

412-945-6600 or 945-5180
Scenery Hill, PA 15360
Megin Harrington, Innkeeper

Gateway Lodge

Amid some of the most magnificent forest scenery east of the Rocky Mountains, this rustic log cabin inn has been called one of the ten best country inns in the U.S. Guests gather around the large stone fireplace in the living room and savor wonderful home-cooked meals by kerosene light. Early American furnishings and an indoor swimming pool delight guests.

 8 rooms, $55/$68 EP
Visa, MC, Amex
credit cards for deposit only

 private and shared baths

 closed Thanksgiving week;
Dec. 22-25

 children accepted (inquire)
no pets

 indoor pool, xc skiing,
bicycling, fishing, summer theatre

 breakfast daily; dinner Tues.—Sun.;
lunch seasonal
wine & liquor available

smoking accepted

conference facilities (45)

I-80, Exit 13 to Rte. 36(N) follow
signs to Cook Forest. Inn is on Rte.
36, ¼ mi. (S) of Cooksburg Bridge.

814-744-8017 (PA: 800-843-6862)
Route 36, Box 125, Cooksburg, PA 16217
The Burney Family, Innkeepers

Glasbern

An ingeniously contemporized Pennsylvania farm with exposed timber, cathedral ceilings, and many windows. The Carriage House rooms have skylights, fireplaces, and whirlpools. With views of the valley and a swimming pool, Glasbern offers deep-country tranquility in a warm and luxurious atmosphere.

 15 rooms, $65/$110 B&B
5 suites, $70/$135 B&B
Visa, MC, Amex

 all private baths, 5 whirlpools

 open year-round

 children accepted
no pets

swimming pool, walking paths,
xc skiing, hot air ballooning,
Hawk Mtn. Sanctuary, antiquing

 breakfast

 smoking allowed

conference facilities (25)

From I-78 take Rte. 100(N) for
.2 mi. to L. at light (W) for .3 mi. to
R. on No. Church St. (N) for .6 mi. to
R. on Pack House Rd. for .8 mi.
to the inn.

215-285-4723
Pack House Rd., R.D. 1, Box 250
Fogelsville, PA 18051-9743
Beth & Al Granger, Innkeepers

Hickory Bridge Farm

A country inn and restaurant located just outside Gettysburg on a family operated, 100-acre farm. Country dining Friday, Saturday, Sunday. The inn is open 7 days a week, B&B. A scenic, quiet setting with a restaurant, a museum, a gift shop, rooms and cottages. A wonderful 'country place.'

 7 rooms, $59/$75 B&B
Visa, MC

 all private baths

 closed Christmas week

 children accepted
no pets

Gettysburg touring, fish,
swim, hike, bike, golf, ski

 breakfast, houseguests
dinner, Fri., Sat., Sun.

 no smoking

wheelchair access
conference facilities

Gettysburg, Rte. 116(W) to Fairfield and R. 3 mi.(N) to Orrtanna.
Or Rte. 977 to Rte. 30(E) for 9 mi.
Turn (S) at Cashtown for 3 mi.
to inn.

717-642-5261
96 Hickory Bridge Rd., Orrtanna, PA 17353
Mary Lynn Martin, Innkeeper

The Inn at Starlight Lake

Since 1909, guests have been drawn to this classic country inn on a beautiful, clear lake in the northeastern Pennsylvania highlands. The congenial atmosphere is warm, inviting, and informal, and there are activities for all seasons, from swimming to cross-country skiing. Lakeside dining offers outstanding French cuisine, which changes with the seasons.

 24 rooms, $110/$140 MAP
1 suite, $330/$345 MAP
Visa, MC

 private and shared baths

 closed Dec. 24, 25;
Apr. 1—15

children accepted
no pets

swimming, boating, tennis,
ice skating, xc skiing, lawn
sports, fishing, golf

 breakfast, lunch, dinner
wine and liquor available

smoking permitted

conference facilites (60)

From NY Rte. 17, Exit 87 (Hancock).
On Rte. 191 (S) 1 mi. to Rte. 370 (W),
turn R. 3 mi. to sign on R. take R, 1 mi.
to inn. From I-81, Exit 62, local roads;
map sent on request.

717-798-2519
Starlight, PA 18461
Judy & Jack McMahon, Innkeepers

The Pine Barn Inn

A part of the history and tradition of Danville for over 100 years, this inn began life first as a barn and then as a riding stable. Today, the restaurant and original rooms still occupy the original barn, with many additional rooms in more recently completed buildings. The restaurant has been renowned for decades for its fresh seafood and homemade pies and pastries.

73 rooms, $36/$60 EP
Visa, Amex, CB, Diners

all private baths

open year-round

children accepted
pets (limited accommodation)

golf, tennis, swimming,
horseback riding, racquetball

breakfast, lunch, dinner
wine and liquor available

non-smoking dining area

wheelchair access (1 room)
conference facilities (50)

From I-80, Exit 33, Rte. 54 (E) 2 mi. to Danville, L. 1st traffic light, signs to Medical Ctr. Inn at entrance to Geisinger Med. Ctr.

717-275-2071
#1 Pine Barn Place, Danville, PA 17821
Martin & Barbara Walzer, Innkeepers

1740 House

An intimate view of the river from a lovely room with a private terrace or balcony is only one of the pleasures at this 18th-century, restored farmhouse on the the banks of the Delaware River. *Newsweek, McCall's, Glamour,* & *Harper's Bazaar* have all listed The 1740 House as one of their 10 favorite inns. The excellent restaurant is open to the public.

23 rooms, $65/$85 B&B
1 suite, $65/$85 B&B
personal checks accepted

all private baths

open year-round

no children
no pets

pool at inn, canoeing,
riding, golf
individual A/C

breakfast daily to houseguests;
dinner, Tues. thru Sat., by res.
BYOB

smoking accepted

wheelchair access (3 rooms)
conference facilities (22)

From NY & NJ use 202 (S) to Rte. 32. From I-95 use New Hope/Yardley exit (N) to New Hope. Lumberville is 7 mi. (N) of New Hope on Rte. 32.

215-297-5661
River Rd. (Hwy. 32), Lumberville, PA 18933
Harry Nessler, Innkeeper

Smithton Inn

A romantic 1763 stone inn located in Lancaster County among the Pennsylvania Dutch. Rooms are large, bright and cheerful with working fireplaces, canopy beds, desks, leather upholstered furniture, Penn. Dutch quilts, candles, chamber music, refrigeration, feather beds (by prior arrangement), books, and reading lamps. Common rooms are warm and inviting with fireplaces.

7 rooms, $55/$105 B&B
1 suite, $130/$160 B&B
Visa, MC, Amex

private baths, some whirlpools

open year-round

children accepted
pets accepted

library, gardens, croquet,
touring, antiques,
Ephrata Cloister

breakfast

no smoking

wheelchair access (1 room)

From north, PA Tpke Exit 21 & Rte. 222 (S). From south, Hwy. 30 to Rte. 222 (N). From north or south, exit Rte. 222 at Rte. 322 (W) for 2.5 mi. to inn.

717-733-6094
900 W. Main St., Ephrata, PA 17522
Dorothy Graybill, Innkeeper

The Sterling Inn

The atmosphere at this family-operated inn has been friendly and unpretentious for over 130 years. In a picture-postcard setting in the Poconos on 106 acres of gardens, lawns, and forest, guests delight in walks along mountain paths with crystal clear streams and a waterfall. Comfortable, attractive rooms and outstanding food make it doubly inviting.

40 rooms, $60/$75 MAP
16 suites, $80/$90 MAP
Visa, MC, Amex

all private baths

open year-round

children accepted
no pets

indoor swimming pool, lake,
tennis, hiking, horseback riding,
golf, xc skiing, horse-drawn
sleigh rides

breakfast, lunch, dinner
wine and liquor available

no smoking in dining area

wheelchair access (2 rooms)
conference facilities (125)

I-84, Exit 6, Rte. 507 (S), 3 mi. to Rte. 191 (S), 3 mi. to inn. I-80 (W) Exit 50, Rte. 191 (N) 25 mi. to inn. I-80 (E) Rte. 380 to Rte. 423 (N), to 191 (N), .5 mi. to inn.

717-676-3311
Rte. 191, South Sterling, PA 18460
Ron & Mary Logan, Innkeepers

Tara—A Country Inn

If you loved the movie *Gone With the Wind*, you will love Tara. Built in 1854, this magnificent mansion reflects the golden days of the antebellum South, with rooms charmingly decorated to recall the grace and grandeur of yester-year. Delightfully different cuisine, from gourmet to family-style, is served in the three totally different restaurants.

 13 rooms, $150 B&B
$198 MAP
Visa, MC

all private baths

 rest. open daily to public exc.
Jan.—mid-Feb. wkends only

not recommended for children
kennels nearby for pets

 bocci, croquet, boating,
golf, bicycling, antiquing,
xc skiing

 breakfast, lunch, dinner
afternoon tea
wine & liquor available

smoking accepted

conference facilities (80)

From I-80, exit 1N, Rte. 18 (N) for 8 mi. Inn is located on (E) side overlooking Lake Shenango.

412-962-3535
3665 Valley View Rd., Box 475, Clark, PA 16113
Jim & Donna Winner, Innkeepers

The Tavern and Lodge

This delightfully old-fashioned restaurant in the fascinating Amish country of northwestern Pennsylvania has been winning followers for over fifty years with bounteous home-style cooking. With the legendary sticky rolls, creamed chicken on a biscuit, and wonderful ham steaks, plus over 25 other selections, this place offers delightful dining in charming surroundings. Guest rooms across the street.

 5 rooms, $41/$44, B&B
tavern—no credit cards
Lodge—Visa, MC

all private baths

 tavern closed July 4,
Dec. 25, Thanksgiving, & Tues.

 children accepted
pets accepted

golf, xc skiing, fishing

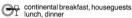 continental breakfast, houseguests
lunch, dinner

smoking accepted

 conference facilities (50)

I-80 E: exit 1S onto Rte. 60 (S), to Rte. 18 (S). (E) on Rte. 208, 6 mi. to inn. I-80 W: Exit 2, (N) to Mercer. (S) on Rte. 158, 9 mi. to inn. I-79: exit Rte. 208 (W), 14 mi. to inn.

412-946-2020
101 N. Market St., New Wilmington, PA 16142
Mary Ellen Durrast, Innkeeper

What Makes Country Inns "Different"?

There are various reasons why one country inn seems different from any other country inn. Here are some of the things, chosen at random, that make country inns special:

Gardens — formal English gardens with topiary bushes, "natural" gardens with wild flowers, vegetable and herb gardens, and everything in between . . .

Displays or use of local arts & crafts — paintings, sculpture, ceramics, baskets, handmade quilts and wallhangings . . .

Collections of artifacts & memorabilia — walking sticks, Revolutionary War firearms, antique pump organs, nickelodeons, ship models, African masks, Oriental tapestries, carved pipes, bells, and other objects from "the old country," farm tools . . .

Museum-quality collections — ancient documents and maps, antique china teapots, rare china, crystal, pewter, "Nanking Cargo" porcelain, Shaker pieces, clocks . . .

Historical references — pictures and books tracing the early history and development of a region, portraits of former owners, printed histories of the inns . . .

Amusing & interesting collections — antique dolls, shoes, & kaleidoscopes, folk art, samplers, hand-cut jigsaw puzzles, stuffed animals . . .

Community involvement — events such as 4th of July celebrations, blueberry or apple festivals, antique car meets, bike or foot races, pumpkin-carving contests, Easter egg hunts, and art shows . . .

Homage to poets — One inn has an Edna St. Vincent Millay Room, where the poet first recited one of her poems; another has many Scottish references, with poems, quotations, and portraits of Robert Burns and Walter Scott and other famous Scots . . .

Miscellaneous — Christmas festivities with huge, festooned trees and all sorts of entertain-ments and events, sometimes including sleigh rides. A 1958 Bentley or a London taxicab for transporting guests to & from the airport . . .

Hotel Manisses, Block Island 4
Inn at Castle Hill, Newport 1
Inntowne, The, Newport 2
Larchwood Inn, Wakefield 3
1661 Inn, Block Island 5

Hotel Manisses

401-466-2421
Spring St. Block Island, RI 02807
The Abrams Family, Innkeepers

Amid the natural beauty of Block Island, this charming Victorian hotel (National Register of Historic Places) is a treasure of unique antique furnishings, stained glass, and many flowers and plants. Dining choices are exceptional, with a gourmet cuisine served inside, on the canopied outdoor deck, or in the glassed-in garden terrace. Reservations suggested.

17 rooms, $48/$235, B&B
Visa, MC, Amex

all private baths

closed Nov. 12—Mar. 30
weekends only, Apr.—May

children over 10 accepted
no pets

swimming, boating, fishing

buffet breakfast, wine & nibble hour for houseguests; dinner
wine & liquor available

smoking accepted

wheelchair access (3 rooms)
conference facilities (80)

By ferry: Providence, Pt. Judith, Newport, RI & New London, Ct.
By air: Newport, Westerly, Providence, RI & New London, Waterford, CT. Contact inn for schedules.

Inn at Castle Hill

401-849-3800
Ocean Drive, Newport, RI 02840
Jens Thillemann, Manager; Paul McEnroe, Innkeeper

Echoes of Newport's Gilded Age are everywhere in this spacious mansion, built in 1874 on 32 acres of secluded shoreline on the edge of Narragansett Bay. Roomy and distinctive guest rooms and baths, with many original furnishings and fittings, breathtaking views of harbor and ocean, and fresh sea breezes beguile guests who enjoy the fine European cuisine and friendly personal service.

15 rooms, $50/$175 B&B
1 suite, $120/$225 B&B
Visa, MC, Amex

private and shared baths

lodging closed Dec. 24, 25
dining rm. closed Dec. 1—Mar. 31

children over 12 accepted
no pets

beaches, walking paths, golf
tennis, bicyling

lunch, Tues.—Sat.; Sun. brunch
dinner, Mon.—Sat.
wine & liquor available

non-smoking dining area

I-95 to Rte. 138 (E) exit downtown Newport to Farewell St., R. to America's Cup Ave. straight to Memorial Blvd., R. on Bellevue Ave., L. on Ocean Ave. 5 mi. (S) of downtown.

The Inntowne

401-846-9200
6 Mary St., Newport, RI 02840
Betty & Paul McEnroe, Innkeepers

This in-town Colonial mansion with a garrison roof is right in the center of bustling Newport, just a block from the water. Rooms are bright and gay with elegant antiques, good reproductions, and paintings. A few steps from the door are beautiful sunsets, towering sailboat masts, quaint and fashionable shops, and many restaurants.

21 rooms, $75/$130 B&B
5 suites, $110/$160 B&B
Visa, MC, Amex

all private baths

closed Dec. 24, 25

children over 12 accepted
no pets

beaches, tennis
boating, mansion touring

continental breakfast
afternoon tea

smoking accepted

conference facilities (15)

Cross Newport bridge, R. at 1st exit sign, R. at bottom of ramp, straight to Thames St. Inn is on corner of Thames and Mary Sts., across from Brick Marketplace.

Larchwood Inn

Watching over the main street of this quaint New England town for 160 years, this grand old house, surrounded by lawns and shaded by stately trees, dispenses hospitality and good food and spirits from early morning to late night. Historic Newport, picturesque Newport, and salty Block Island are a short ride away.

 19 rooms, $30/$80 EP
Visa, MC, Amex, Discov

private and shared baths

open year-round

 children accepted
pets allowed

ocean swimming, fishing, golf, tennis, historic touring bicycling, boating

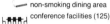 breakfast, lunch, dinner
wine and liquor available

non-smoking dining area

conference facilities (125)

From I-95 (N), Exit 92 to Rte. 78 (E) to Rte. 1 (N) to Main St. Wakefield. From I-95 (S), Rte. 4 (S) to Rte. 1 (S).

401-783-5454
521 Main St., Wakefield, RI 02879
Francis & Diann Browning, Innkeepers

The 1661 Inn

With glorious views of the ocean from most of the guest room decks, the long, wooden, canopied seaward deck, and the oceanview dining room, this distinctly Colonial inn takes full advantage of its island setting. Extravagant breakfasts and hearty New England cuisine satisfies appetites stimulated by fresh air and exercise.

 23 rooms, $60/$215 B&B
Visa, MC, Amex

 private and shared baths

open year-round

 children accepted
no pets

swimming, boating, fishing, bicycling, lawn games

 breakfast; dinner, summer only
wine and nibble hour
wine & liquor available

 smoking accepted

 conference facilities (80)

By ferry: Providence, Pt. Judith, Newport, RI, and New London, CT. By air: Newport, Westerly, Providence, RI and New London, Waterford, CT. Contact inn for schedules.

401-466-2421 or 466-2063
Spring St., Block Island, RI 02807
The Abrams Family, Innkeepers

The Wonderful World Of Country Inn Cookery

Just as every country inn has its own individual style in furnishings and decoration, so, too, is its cuisine different and distinctive from every other inn. There are those who adhere to the principle that simple, wholesome, home-cooked, family-style meals, probably with a definite regional flavor, are the best. Others offer more sophisticated French, European, or even exotic ethnic cuisine choices. Nowhere will you find standardized hotel food.

The cook might be the innkeeper himself or herself, who also might be a graduate of the Cordon Bleu or the Culinary Institute of America—or just a naturally great cook. Some innkeepers are master chefs. Some inns hire well-known chefs, who give a special patina to their culinary presentations.

Dining rooms are usually arranged restaurant-style with small tables, but there are still a few places where meals are served family-style and guests sit together at a large table where everyone joins in the conversation. Sometimes meals are served on porches or terraces with lovely views, or in courtyards, patios, and gardens.

With the growing interest in wines, more inns are widening their selection and can boast extensive cellars of fine wines. Bed and breakfast inns often offer complimentary before-dinner

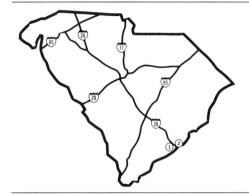

Guilds Inn, Mount Pleasant   2
36 Meeting Street, Charleston   1

Guilds Inn

In the beautiful old village of Mt. Pleasant, a suburb of Charleston, this restored (1888) Colonial-style clapboard building offers friendly hospitality in rooms furnished with fine antique reproductions. The nationally acclaimed "Supper at Seven" restaurant serves superb dinners, and nearby Charleston Harbor, ocean, and beach offer myriad diversions.

 4 rooms, $85/$100 B&B
2 suites, $125 B&B
Visa, MC, Amex

 all private baths

 open year-round

 children accepted
no pets

 bicycling, beach, tennis
golf, fishing,
Charleston nearby

 dinner, Tues.—Sat.
7 p.m. seating, fixed-price
wine & liquor available

 no smoking in dining room

 wheelchair access (6 rooms)
conference facilities (20)

From Charleston: Rte. 17 (N) or 701 (E) to Mt. Pleasant. On Coleman Blvd., 6th traffic light R. fork to Whilden St. (S).2 mi. to Venning St. R. 1 block to inn.

803-881-0510
101 Pitt St., Mt. Pleasant, SC 29464
Guilds Hollowell, Owner; John & Amy Malik, Innkeepers

36 Meeting Street

This authentically and beautifully furnished 1740 private home in the heart of Charleston's historic district is included in tours of historic buildings. However, the hospitality is strictly 20th century, with fully stocked kitchenette suites and all the amenities of modern life, including a morning newspaper, fresh fruit and flowers. Perfect for private-home tours, Spoleto U.S.A., historic sites, and museums.

 2 suites, $65/$85 B&B
no credit cards
personal checks accepted

 both private baths

 closed Dec. 23—27

children accepted
no pets

historic sites, house tours, theater, art, shops, private gardens, antiques, carriage rides

 complimentary full breakfast stocked in kitchenette

smoking accepted

From I-26 and Rte. 17 (N) exit Meeting St. downtown (S). From 17 (S) exit at Lockwood Blvd. to Broad St. R. onto Meeting St. (S). Inn on (E) side of Meeting St.

803-722-1034
36 Meeting St., Charleston, SC 29401
David & Suzanne Redd, Innkeepers

---

wines and other refreshments, while some full-service inns follow the custom of having a get-acquainted cocktail hour before serving dinner.

Afternoon teas and Sunday brunches are opportunities to display all sorts of marvelous pastries and wonderful specialties and are usually served to the public as well as houseguests.

Vegetable and herb gardens are an integral part of a number of inns, which take great pride in the freshness and flavor of their produce. And nothing could be fresher for a guest than the fish he caught that afternoon and had cooked for his dinner that night—which is possible to do at a few inns.

(For a sampling of the kind of food you might find at a country inn, turn the page.)

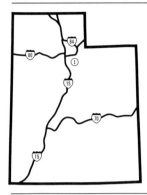

Homestead, The, Midway 1

The Homestead

This venerable inn has a 100-year history of offering hospitality amid 60 acres of lawns, fields, fountains, and panoramic views of magnificent mountains. In addition to a wide range of impeccably furnished guest rooms and exceptional dining, there is a remarkable array of activities at this year-round resort, including hot indoor and outdoor mineral baths.

 74 rooms, $59/$175 EP
9 suites, $165/$225, EP
Visa, MC, Amex, Discov

 all private baths

 open year-round

children accepted
no pets

 xc & downhill skiing, golf, indoor & outdoor swimming, horseback riding

breakfast, lunch, dinner
wine & liquor available

smoking accepted

 wheelchair access (1 room)
conference facilities (120)

From Salt Lake City: I-80 (E) to Silver Creek Junction. (S) on Rte. 40/189. In Heber City (W) at Rte. 113 (Midway Lane) 5 mi. to Homestead Dr.

800-327-7220; (in Utah) 800-345-7220
P.O. Box 99, 700 N. Homestead Dr., Midway, UT 84049
Gerald & Carole Sanders, Owners;
Britt Mathwich, Innkeeper

Country Inn Food Sampler

Colonial corn and mussel chowder, cured salmon, rabbit in puff pastry, half duckling in apple and peppercorn sauce, baked grapefruit with a sautéed chicken liver, romaine soup, local fish baked in wine, leg of lamb with fresh rosemary, lobster pie, double-thick lamb chops, baked ham with peach glaze . . .

Homemade Georgia crackers with fresh fruit salad, Louisiana chicken with artichoke hearts and almonds, roast duckling with orange-cranberry sauce, sautéed mountain trout, vegetable strudel, steak and kidney pie, roast squab with fresh peaches, veal with pomegranate wine, crayfish fritters . . .

Carolina quail with savory cabbage, fillet of beef on fried eggplant, tomato cups with fresh corn, low country squash pie, local channel bass in puff pastry, smoked ham, grits, and cornbread, stuffed pork chops, Midwestern fish boils, cooked outside in huge iron cauldrons over a roaring fire and served with coleslaw, fresh-baked bread, and cherry pie.

Desserts might be fudge walnut cake, pistachio cake, pecan pie, hot gingerbread with lemon sauce, triple mousse cake with whipped cream, deep dish apple pie, fruit cobbler, indian pudding, sour cream apple pie, fresh figs filled with white chocolate mousse, homemade angel food cake with strawberries and whipped cream.

Some breakfast possibilities: Crêpes Suzette, blueberry pancakes, herbed eggs with cheese and mushrooms, fresh fruit, sausage or ham biscuits, German apple pancakes, eggs Benedict, french toast with strawberries and whipped cream, cheddar egg bake with Dijon mustard and broccoli, fresh-baked muffins with quince jelly, poached pear in caramel sauce, kiwi with puréed raspberries.

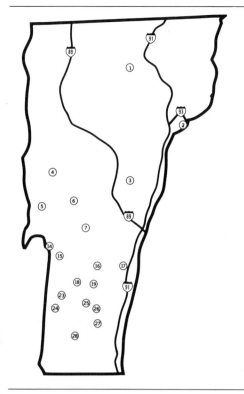

Birch Hill Inn

On a back road away from busy village streets, among fabulous white birches, this inn has the feeling of a gracious home and quiet, peaceful retreat. Each cheerfully decorated room has views of surrounding mountains, farms, and gardens. Hearty breakfasts and fine country dinners are among the pleasures to be found here.

5 rooms, $96/$106 B&B
1 cottage, $96 B&B
Visa, MC

all private baths

closed Nov. 1—Dec. 26
Apr. 10—May 30

children over 6 accepted
no pets

pool, trout pond, walking & xc ski trails, antiquing, summer theatre

breakfast & tea; dinner for guests Mon., Tues., Fri. & Sat. wine available

smoking accepted in living room

In Manchester Center, junction of Rtes. 7A & 30, take Rte. 30 (N) for 2.7 mi. to Manchester West Rd., go L. (S) for ¾ of mi.

802-362-2761
West Rd., P.O. Box 346, Manchester, VT 05254
Pat & Jim Lee, Innkeepers

Blueberry Hill

Winter at Blueberry Hill means snow, skiing, roaring fires, hearty soups, and snuggling under warm quilts; summer means loafing under an apple tree, picking blueberries, floating in the spring-fed pond, and dining simply but elegantly in the candlelit communal dining room. There's much more at this restored 1813 farmhouse, tucked away in the Green Mountains.

12 rooms, $68/$135 MAP
Visa, MC

all private baths

open May—Oct., Dec.—Mar.
closed Dec. 25

children accepted
no pets

xc skiing, hiking, swimming

breakfast; dinner by reservation

no smoking

wheelchair access (1 room)
conference facilities (100)

U.S. Rte. 7 (N) to Brandon, Vt. Rte. 73 (E), to Forest Rd. #32, take L. for 4 mi.

802-247-6735 or 800-448-0707
Goshen, VT 05733
Tony Clark, Innkeeper

The Governor's Inn

This may be the ultimate experience at an elegant Victorian country inn. From potpourri-scented air to the soft strains of classical music to the beautifully kept family heirlooms, attention is given to every detail of aesthetic pleasure and comfort. National recognition and awards for excellence and superb cuisine only add to the warm hospitality.

 8 rooms, $170/$180 MAP
Visa, MC

all private baths

closed Apr. & Nov.

 no children
no pets

skiing, antiquing, golf, boating, fishing

 breakfast, dinner
afternoon tea
wine & liquor available

smoking restricted

Ludlow is located at junction of Rtes. 100 & 103. Inn is (S) on Rte. 103, just off village green.

802-228-8830
86 Main St., Ludlow, VT 05149
Charlie & Deedy Marble, Innkeepers

Historic Brookside Farms

This magnificent 200-year-old Greek Revival mansion is an architect's dream, where antique furnishings, paintings, and music abound. Skiers have only to step out the door to enjoy 300 acres of trails and meadow skiing. The farm provides wholesome food for the table, with beef and lambs and vast vegetable gardens. Three generations of innkeepers welcome guests to this homey setting.

 5 rooms, $65/$125 B&B
1 suite $135/$170 B&B
no credit cards

private & shared baths

open year-round

 children accepted
no pets

hiking, xc skiing, boating, fishing, golf, tennis, horseback riding

 breakfast, dinner—houseguests
lunch by request
wine available with dinner

smoking restricted

 wheelchair access (1 room)
conference facilities (50)

From I-87 (N), exit 20 (Glens Falls). L. on Rte. 9 to Rte. 149 (E) to Rte. 4 (E) to Rte. 22A (N) on 22A for 13 mi. From I-89 (N) exit White River Junction, Rte. 4 (W) to 22A (N).

802-948-2727
Route 22A, Orwell, VT 05760
Joan & Murray Korda, Innkeepers

The Inn at Sawmill Farm

What was a wonderful barn in 1797 on a hillside overlooking a tiny village is now a beautiful and elegant country inn, filled with antiques, English chintzes, brass and copper period pieces, and a walk-in fireplace. Separate cottages have fireplaces. The American-Continental cuisine is sumptuous and the wine cellar outstanding.

 2 rooms, $220/$250 MAP
22 suites $240/$265 MAP
no credit cards

all private baths

closed Dec. 1—Dec. 15

 children over 10 accepted
no pets—kennel nearby

pool, tennis, trout ponds, xc & downhill skiing, golf, horseback riding

 breakfast & dinner
wine & liquor available

smoking accepted

 conference facilities (42)

From I-91 (N) Exit 2 (Brattleboro) (W) on Rte. 9 to Rte. 100. (N) on Rte. 100, 5 mi. to inn. Or (N) on U.S. Rte. 7 to Bennington, VT. (E) on Rte. 9 to Rte. 100.

802-464-8131
Country Club Rd., Box 367, West Dover, VT 05356
Rodney, Brill, & Ione Williams, Innkeepers

The Inn at Weathersfield

Congeniality and caring make this 18th-century stagecoach stop special. With its working beehive oven, 12 fireplaces, nooks for quiet conversation, fitness center and sauna, and many guest rooms with working fireplaces, this beautiful inn satisfies many interests. A gourmet kitchen, horse-drawn sleigh and carriage, a pond, and a tennis court are a few of the attractions.

 10 rooms, $150/$160 MAP
2 suites, $200 MAP
Visa, MC, Amex

all private baths

open year-round

 children over 8 accepted
pets accepted with prior notice

tennis, fishing, swimming golf, skating, carriage & sleigh rides, sauna & fitness rooms

 breakfast, dinner
high tea
wine & liquor available

smoking restricted

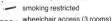 wheelchair access (3 rooms)
conference facilities (50)

From I-91 (N), Exit 7 (Springfield), Rte. 11 (W) to Rte. 106 (N). Inn 5 mi. on left. From I-91 (S) Exit 8, Rte. 131 (W) to Rte. 106 (S). Inn is 4 mi. on right.

802-263-9217
Route 106, Box 165, Weathersfield, VT 05151
Mary Louise & Ron Thorburn, Innkeepers

Inn on the Common

With the ambience of a sophisticated country house hotel, this inn offers an outstanding cuisine, created by 3 chefs, and an excellent wine cellar, including grand crus and many single vineyard bottlings. The lovely and comfortable guest rooms, elegantly decorated with antiques and artworks, are spread among a compound of 3 restored Federal houses.

 17 rooms, $150/$230 MAP
Visa, MC

 all private baths

 open year-round

 children accepted
pets accepted

 pool, tennis court, gardens, xc skiing, golf, lake, trails

 breakfast & dinner
wine & liquor available

 no smoking in dining room

 conference facilities (20)

From I-91 (N), Exit 21, Rte. 2 (W) to Rte. 15 (W). In Hardwick, Rte. 14 (N) 7 mi., turn R., 3 mi. to inn. From I-91 (S) Exit 26, Rte. 58 (W), Rte. 14 (S) 12 mi. to marked L. turn.

802-586-9619
Main Street, Craftsbury Common, VT 05827
Michael & Penny Schmitt, Innkeepers

The Middlebury Inn

This has been a community landmark since 1827 (National Register of Historic Places), its classic red brick, white shutters, and striped yellow canopy presiding colorfully over this historic, picturesque New England college town. Beautifully decorated with antiques and memorabilia, the feeling in the many comfortable sitting areas and the spacious West Porch is informal and friendly..

 65 rooms, $76/$120 EP
4 suites, $116 EP
Visa, MC, Amex

 all private baths

 open year-round

 children welcome
pets in motel section

 swimming, golf, tennis, hiking

breakfast, lunch, dinner
Sun. brunch
wine & liquor available

smoking accepted

 wheelchair access (15 rooms)
conference facilities (50)

Inn is on U.S. Rte. 7. From I-87 (N) Exit 20, Rte. 149 (E) to Rte. 4 (E) (N) to Rte. 30 (N) to Middlebury. Inn is in village center.

802-388-4961 or 800-842-4666
P.O. Box 798, Courthouse Square, Rte. 7.
Middlebury, VT 05753
Frank & Jane Emanuel, Innkeepers

Middletown Springs Inn

Dominating the green of the small, rural Vermont village, this 1879 Victorian mansion displays Victoriana in its best light with decorations and beautiful antiques of the period. The big country kitchen produces delectable breakfasts and hearty, savory dinners. Ask about special weekend events and holiday festivities, particularly the Christmas sleigh rides and treasures hunts.

 10 rooms, $110/$140 MAP
$70/$90 B&B
Visa, MC

 8 private, 1 shared baths

 open year-round

 no facilities for children under 6
no pets

library, xc skiing, golf, swimming, antiquing

breakfast & dinner
wine & liquor available

smoking restricted

 conference facilities (10)

From Rte. 4, Exit 6 to Rte. 4A (W) .1 mi. to Rte. 133 (S) 11.5 mi. to inn. From Rte. 7 (W) take Rte. 30 (N) (Manchester Center) to Poultney, Rte. 140 (E) 9 mi. to inn.

802-235-2198
On the Green, Box 1068, Middletown Springs, VT 05757
Jane & Steve Sax, Innkeepers

Mountain Top Inn and Resort

Commanding a spectacular lake and mountain view on a 1,000-acre estate, this inn offers a complete resort experience. Included in the rates are horseback riding, tennis, heated pool, sailing, fishing, pitch 'n' putt golf, cross-country skiing and lessons, ice skating and skates, horse drawn sleigh rides, and much more. Attractive, congenial surroundings, and fine dining complete the picture.

 33 rooms, $152/$330 MAP
19 cottages, $184 MAP
Visa, MC, Amex

 all private baths

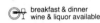 open year-round

children welcome
no pets—kennels nearby

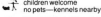 full resort—xc skiing, skating, sleigh rides, swimming, horseback riding, sailing, golf, tennis

breakfast, lunch, dinner
wine & liquor available

no smoking in dining room

conference facilities (180)

Chittenden is 10 mi. (NE) of Rutland. (N) on Rte. 7 or (E) on Rte. 4 from Rutland, follow state signs to "Mountain Top Inn."

802-483-2311 or 800-445-2100
Mountain Top Rd. Chittenden, VT 05737
William Wolfe, Innkeeper

Old Newfane Inn

Creating new attention for this 200-year-old hostelry, chef-owner Eric Weindl's French-Swiss cuisine has earned kudos from many food critics and delighted guests. He prides himself on the freshness and quality of his provisions. The low-ceilinged candlelit dining room offers the perfect dining experience. Pleasant guest rooms evoke a feeling of yesteryear.

 6 rooms, $85 B&B
2 suites, $125 B&B
personal checks accepted

all private baths

closed Apr. & Nov.

 children over 12 welcome
no pets

 downhill & xc skiing, hiking, swimming, golf

continental breakfast, dinner
wine & liquor available

smoking permitted

conference facilities (16)

I-91 (N), Exit 2 (Brattleboro). Follow signs to Manchester on Rte. 30 (N). Inn is on Rte. 30 in Newfane, across the village green.

802-365-4427
Court Street, P.O. Box 101, Newfane, VT 05345
Eric & Gundy Weindl, Innkeepers

Rabbit Hill Inn

Full of whimsical and charming surprises, this 1825 Federal-period inn has been lavished with love and attention. Many guest rooms with fireplaces and lacy canopied beds, soft music, candlelit gourmet meals, and turn-down service make this an enchanting hideaway in a tiny restored village over-looking the mountains.

16 rooms, $130/$180 MAP
2 suites, $160/$180 MAP
Visa, MC

all private baths

closed Apr. & 1st 2 weeks of Nov.

 children over 12 accepted
no pets

 water & lawn sports, hiking, skiing, antiquing, golf

breakfast & dinner
wine & liquor available

no smoking

conference facilities (40)

From I-91 (N or S), Exit 19 to I-93 (S). Exit 1, R. on Rte. 18 (S), 7 mi. to inn. From I-93 (N), Exit 44, L. on Rte. 18 (N), 2 mi. to inn.

802-748-5168
Route 18, Lower Waterford, VT 05848
John & Maureen Magee, Innkeepers

Rowell's Inn

This 1820 stagecoach stop (National Register of Historic Places) continues to welcome weary travelers with a brand of hospitality those early guests never enjoyed. Filled with antiques and memorabilia, cozy fireplaces, an English-style pub, and a kitchen overflowing with intriguing things, this inn offers guests hearty, toothsome dishes, and casual, homey comfort in authentic period surroundings.

5 rooms, $120/$140 MAP
no credit cards

all private baths

closed Apr. & 1st 2 weeks of Nov.

 children over 12 accepted
no pets

 skiing, golf, tennis, fishing, bicycling, hiking

breakfast & dinner for houseguests only
wine & beer available

smoking accepted

The inn is on Rte. 11 (an east/west rte., connecting Rtes. 7 & I-91. The inn is 7 mi. (W) of Chester and 7 mi. (E) of Londonderry.

802-875-3658
RR #1, Box 269, Simonsville, VT 05143
Beth & Lee Davis, Innkeepers

Shire Inn

This inn overlooks a river with a wooden bridge in a pristine Vermont village (National Register of Historic Places). One of the most attractive historic homes is this 1832 Federal brick building, with its fanlight and black shutters. With five working fireplaces, spiral staircase, high ceilings, canopied beds, and many books, this inn offers elegant hospitality, along with exceptional meals.

6 rooms, $65/$95 B&B
Visa, MC

all private baths

open year-round

 children over 6 accepted
no pets

 xc & downhill skiing, skating, sleigh rides, bicycling, swimming canoeing, antiquing

breakfast & dinner
wine & beer available

no smoking

I-89, Vt. Exit 2 (Sharon) L. for 300 yds., R. on Rte. 14 (N). R. onto Rte. 110 (N), 13 mi. to Chelsea. From I-91, Exit 14, L. onto Rte. 113 (N/W) to Chelsea.

802-685-3031
Main Street, Box 37, Chelsea, VT 05038
James & Mary Lee Papa, Innkeepers

Three Mountain Inn

This beautifully restored c. 1780 Colonial has wide planked pine walls and an original Dutch oven fireplace in the living room, lots of books in the library, and fireplaces in the two cheerful dining rooms, where delicious meals are served. Guest rooms are attractive and comfortable, and the atmosphere is casual and relaxed.

 15 rooms, $130/$180 MAP
no credit cards

 13 private, 1 shared baths

closed Apr.; Nov. 3—24 & Dec. 1—14

no children
no pets

 swimming pool, hiking, bicycling, tennis, golf, horseback riding

 breakfast & dinner
wine & liquor available

smoking restricted

conference facilities (45)

Jamaica is located on Rte. 30, ½ hr. (E) of Manchester (U.S. Rte. 7) and ½ hr. (W) of Brattleboro, (I-91, Exit 2).

802-874-4140
180 Main St., P.O. Box 180, Jamaica, VT 05343
Charles & Elaine Murray, Innkeepers

Vermont Marble Inn

Recently restored to its original Italianate Victorian grandeur, with 7 hand-carved marble fireplaces, high ornate ceilings, and etched-glass windows, this magnificent marble mansion is indeed a showplace. The atmosphere is comfortable, casual, and warm. Breakfasts are lavish and the gourmet cuisine has earned rave reviews, including 3 stars and 3 diamonds.

 8 rooms, $65/$95 B&B
5 suites, $98/$108 B&B
Visa, MC, Amex

 all private baths

open year-round

children welcome
no pets

 water sports, skiing, golf, bicycling, horseback riding

 breakfast—houseguests only
dinner, Sun. brunch—public invited
wine & liquor available

smoking accepted

conference facilities (30)

I-87, Exit 20. Rte. 149 (W) to Rte. 4 (N), Exit 2 in VT, follow sign to Fair Haven. Straight down street to town green.

802-265-8383
On the Town Green, Fair Haven, VT 05743
Bea & Richard Taube, Shirley Stein, Innkeepers

The Village Inn at Landgrove

The principle of "Vermont continuous architecture" extended this original 1840 farmhouse into the rambling inn it is today. It is in a true country inn setting, tucked into a valley in the mountains, with gravel roads and a town population of 200. There's candlelit, fireside dining, and a mix of activities and fun for all ages at this informal, engaging country inn.

 20 rooms, $45/$70 B&B
Visa, MC

private & shared baths

closed Apr. 1—Jun. 1
Oct. 20—Dec. 20

children welcome
no pets

 tennis courts, heated pool, platform tennis, hay & sleigh rides, golf, xc & downhill skiing

 breakfast & dinner
wine & liquor available

smoking accepted

conference facilities (40)

I-91 (N), Exit 2 (Brattleboro). Rte. 30 (N), R. onto Rte. 11. L. at signs for Village Inn, bear L. in village of Peru. From Rte. 7 (N), (E) in Manchester on Rte. 11. Continue as above.

802-824-6673
R.D. 1, Box 215, Weston Rd.,
Landgrove, Londonderry, VT 05148
Jay & Kathy Snyder, Innkeepers

West Mountain Inn

Llamas and African violets are only two of the delightful surprises at this happy, relaxed country inn, high on a hill above the Battenkill River. In addition to Wes Carlson's herd of llamas and the custom of presenting guests with a lovely African violet, there are cheerful rooms, exceptional New England country cuisine, and a spirit of genuine warmth and hospitality.

 12 rooms, $115/$145 MAP
3 suites, $170 MAP
Visa, MC, Amex

 13 private, 1 shared baths

open year-round

children welcome
no pets

 hiking, river swimming, tubing, fishing, canoeing, xc & downhill skiing, tennis, theatre, museums

 breakfast & dinner
wine & liquor available

smoking restricted

wheelchair access (1 room)
conference facilities (50)

Rt. 7 (N), Exit 3. Take access road to end, R. on Rte. 7A into Arlington. L. on Rte. 313 for .5 mi. L. on River Rd. to inn.

802-375-6516
Box 481, Rte. 313 & River Rd., Arlington, VT 05250
Mary Ann & Wes Carlson, Innkeepers

Windham Hill Inn

On 150 acres, threaded by rock walls and bounded by infinite, magnificent views across the hills, this inn is almost a feeling more than a place. Offering peace and seclusion, the friendly, unobtrusive innkeepers welcome guests to this charming retreat, with its antique shoe collection, sparkling rooms, memorable meals, and closeness to nature.

 15 rooms, $150/$170 MAP
Visa, MC, Amex

 breakfast & dinner
wine & liquor available

all private baths

smoking restricted

closed Apr. to mid-May,
early Nov.

conference facilities (30)

children over 12 accepted
no pets

I-91 (N), Exit 2 (Brattleboro).
Rte. 30 (N) for 21.5 mi. R. on
Windham Rd. 1.5 mi. to inn.

802-874-4080
R.R. 1, Box 44, West Townshend, VT 05359
Ken & Linda Busteed, Innkeepers

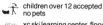 xc ski learning center, flood lit
skating pond, downhill skiing,
summer concerts, hiking

Tennis Anyone?

There are usually places to go, things to do, and sights to see in the vicinity of most country inns, and the inns will have suggestions and maps for all sorts of activities, scenic drives, and sightseeing, from nature walks to nearby historic sites to the best outlet shopping. Tennis courts, swimming pools, and sometimes golf courses are standard at resort inns. Many other forms of diversion are offered at various inns. Here is an idea of the kinds of recreation or entertainment you might find on the grounds or under the auspices of a country inn.

Near water there could be fishing, sailing, rowboating, canoeing, kayaking, paddle boating, rafting, waterskiing, and tubing. A couple of innkeepers have Coast Guard captain's licenses and take guests out in their boats. Others have boats for the use of their guests for fishing, excursions, and sightseeing.

In ski country, sometimes there are groomed and marked ski and nature trails leading from front doors into woods, where deer, moose, fox, mink, bobcats, raccoons, or maybe even a bear might be glimpsed. Some inns have their own ski shops with lessons and rental equipment. These might also have tobogganing, sledding, and ice skating.

Western ranches have horses and trail rides, as do a few inns in the South and East. Farms have animals for petting, feeding, and watching; some guests like to flex their muscles at haying time, tossing and stacking bales of hay.

Guided or unguided wildflower, birdwatching, and nature walks might include a picnic beside a forest stream. Some inns provide a basket of goodies for a picnic lunch on a remote beach, by a waterfall, or to break a mountain hike or a bicycle ride on back roads. There are inn-to-inn programs for hikers and bikers.

A couple of inns feature hot-air balloon rides, either from the inn grounds or nearby.

Some on-premises activities include English croquet, shuffleboard, lawn bowling, paddle tennis, pitch 'n' putt golf, volleyball, horseshoes, ping-pong, pool or billiards, fitness centers for aerobic exercise, Nordic track exercisers, stationary bicycles, rowing machines, barre, weights, hot tubs, saunas, spas with mineral springs, massages, and facials.

For rainy days, some inns have VCR's and film libraries, puzzles, board games, and libraries of all sorts of books and magazines. Some inns offer evening entertainment with lovely music programs—musicians playing original instruments and tunes from the 1800s, or chamber music and soloists, or sometimes impromptu recitals by a talented guest who sits down at the baby grand or picks up a guitar. A few innkeepers are accomplished musicians in their own right. A Canadian inn offers local color with films about the area, storytellers, singers and fiddlers, and square dances. Another Canadian inn holds sugaring-off parties in March.

And then there is the inn that has created a sylvan glade where guests can sit and commune with nature. And there are lots of porches with rocking chairs—sometimes all the recreation or entertainment a guest desires is to sit and rock and watch the world go by.

VIRGINIA

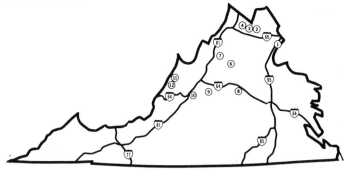

Ashby Inn, Paris 3
Graves' Mountain Lodge, Syria 6
Inn at Gristmill Square,
 Warm Springs 11
Jordan Hollow Farm Inn, Stanley 7
L'Auberge Provençale,
 White Post 4
Maple Hall, Lexington 10
Meadow Lane Lodge,
 Warm Springs 12
Morrison House, Alexandria 1
Prospect Hill, Trevilians 8
Red Fox Inn & Tavern,
 Middleburg 2
Trillium House, Nellysford 9

The Ashby Inn

This 1829 inn finds its character in the small village of Paris and its heart in the kitchen. The views from guest rooms or dining patio are wonderful in every direction. The menu changes daily, ranging from home-cured salmon gravlaks or local wild mushrooms on toast to jumbo lump crabcakes or duckling with turnips.

 6 rooms, $80/$115 B&B
Visa, MC, Amex

 private & shared baths

 closed Jan. 1; July 4;
Dec. 24 & 25

 children over 10 accepted
no pets

crocquet, bocci, horseshoes
horseback riding, golf, fishing
hiking, antiquing

 breakfast; dinner, Wed.—Sat.,
Sun. brunch
wine & liquor available

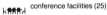 no smoking in guest rooms

 conference facilities (25)

From Wash, D.C.: Rte. 66 (W) to Exit 5—Rte. 17 (N), 7.5 mi. L. on Rte. 701 for .5 mi. Or Rte. 50 (W) thru Middleburg; 3 mi. beyond Upperville, L. just after yellow light (Rte. 759).

703-592-3900
Rte. 1, Box 2A, Paris, VA 22130
John & Roma Sherman, Innkeepers

Graves Mountain Lodge

This Blue Ridge Mountain rustic paradise offers complete resort facilities as well as gracious Southern hospitality and good home-cooked food, like country-fried chicken, baked ham, corn pudding, and hot fudge cake. So many fun things to do here, from experiencing the great natural beauty all around to sightseeing and touring to just relaxing and enjoying the rustic serenity.

 53 rooms/cabins, $74/$144 AP
Visa, MC

 private & shared baths

 closed Dec. to Mar.

 children accepted
pets accepted in some rooms

swimming, tennis, nature walks
hiking, fishing, basketball

 breakfast, lunch, dinner
wine available

smoking allowed

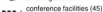 wheelchair access (38 rooms)
conference facilities (100)

From Madison, VA, U.S. Rte. 29, take Rte. 231 (N) for 7 mi. to L. at Greystone Service Sta. Turn L. on Rte. 670 for 3 mi. to Syria Gen'l. Store. Continue .5 mi. to lodge on L.

703-923-4231
General Delivery, Syria, VA 22743
Jim & Rachel Graves, Innkeepers

The Inn at Gristmill Square

On a designated historic site, a 1771 gristmill and a blacksmith's shop are among the cluster of restored 19th-century buildings comprising this handsome inn. Guest rooms are tastefully furnished in both traditional and contemporary decor; many have working fireplaces. Exceptional dining and the many attractions of the Allegheny Mountains and spa country draw visitors from afar.

 8 rooms, $75/$85 EP
6 suites, $75/$105 EP
Visa, MC

 all private baths

 open year-round

 children welcome
pets welcome

swimming pool, 3 tennis courts,
sauna, golf, horseback riding,
hiking, fishing, skiing, ice skating

continental breakfast & dinner
lunch—limited days; MAP available
wine & liquor available

smoking allowed

conference facilities (45)

From (N) on Rte. U.S. 220 turn L. (W) on Rte. 619 (small state marker) for .3 mi. to inn on L. From (S) on Rte. 220, R. (W) on Rte. 619.

703-839-2231
Rte. 619, P.O. Box 359, Warm Springs, VA 24484
The McWilliams Family, Innkeepers

Jordan Hollow Farm

Here is an inn on a 200-acre restored Colonial horse farm where German Holsteiner and Norwegian Fjord horses are bred. Guest rooms have sun porches and rocking chairs, and organic gardens supply much of the "country continental" menu. There are walking trails and riding trails for both beginners and experienced riders, as well as riding and driving clinics.

 16 rooms, $65/$75 EP
1 suite, $75/$85 EP
Visa, MC, Diners, CB

all private baths

open year-round

 well-behaved children welcome
pets accepted in kennel

horseback riding, pub/game
rooms, walking trails, hiking,
swimming, canoeing

all meals
wine & liquor available

smoking allowed

wheelchair access (1 room)
conference facilities (34)

Luray, VA, Rte. 340 (S) for 6 mi.
to L. onto Rte. 624. L. on Rte. 68©
over bridge & R. on Rte. 626 for
.4 mi. to inn on R.

703-778-2209
Route 2, Box 375, Stanley, VA 22851
Marley & Jetze Beers, Innkeepers

L'Auberge Provençale

A warm "south of France" breath blows over this eclectic and sophisticated country inn, with its renowned "cuisine moderne Provençale" by French master chef/owner Alain Borel, who grows his own vegetables, herbs and spices. Charming guest rooms and the bucolic setting in the hunt country of northern Virginia offer a special experience for discerning guests.

 6 rooms, $100/$140 B&B
Visa, MC

all private baths

closed Jan. 1 thru Feb. 10

 children over 9
no pets

 horseback riding, antiquing, golf,
tennis, canoeing, sightseeing

breakfast & dinner
wine & liquor available

smoking allowed

conference facilities (30)

On Rte. 340 (S), 1 mi. (S) of Rte.
50; 20 mi. (W) of Middleburg,
9 mi. (E) of Winchester, VA

703-837-1375
Route 340, P.O. Box 119, White Post, VA 22663
Celeste & Alain Borel, Innkeepers

Maple Hall

A member of the Historic Inns of Lexington, this 1850 plantation home on 56 rolling acres offers guests a lovely place for recreation, exploring historic sites, or just relaxing. There are walking trails, a swimming pool for a splash after tennis, fish in the ½-acre pond, fireplaces in attractive guest rooms, and historic Lexington is a short drive away.

 14 rooms, $75/$90 B&B
1 suite, $90/$115 B&B
Visa, MC

all private baths

open year-round

 no pets

tennis, pool, croquet, fishing,
walking paths, golf, canoeing,
hiking, museums, historic sites

breakfast, houseguests
dinner daily
wine & liquor available

smoking somewhat restricted

wheelchair access (1 room)
conference facilities (20)

I-81 Exit 53 to Rte. 11 (N). Inn is
(E) of the Interstate.

703-463-2044
11 No. Main St., Lexington, VA 24450
Peter Meredith Family, Owners;
Don Fredenburg, Innkeeper

Meadow Lane Lodge

With 2 miles of a scenic private trout and bass stream rippling through its 1600 acres of mountain forests and meadows, this is one of the most unusual inns to be found anywhere. Wildflowers, wildlife, birdlife, and domestic animals galore add to the enjoyment of this beautiful, peaceful estate, a rarity in today's rapidly expanding world.

 11 rooms, $89/$95 B&B
3 suites, $98/$220 B&B
Visa, MC, Amex

all private baths, 1 Jacuzzi

closed Jan., Feb., Mar.

 children over 6 welcome
pets require prior approval

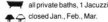 tennis, fishing, swimming,
croquet, hiking, mtn. biking,
Cascades Golf Course

breakfast for houseguests
sherry available

no smoking in dining room

wheelchair access (2 rooms)
conference facilities (16)

From Staunton, Rte. 254 (W) to
Buffalo Gap; Rte. 42 to Millboro
Sprgs. Rte. 39 to lodge. From
Roanoke, Rte. 220 (N) to junction
Rte. 39 (W) 4 mi. to lodge.

703-839-5959
Star Route A, Box 110, Warm Springs, VA 24484
Philip & Cathy Hirsh, Innkeepers

Morrison House

800-367-0800/703-533-1808 (VA)/703-838-8000 (local)
116 S. Alfred St., Alexandria, VA 22314
Robert Morrison, Owner/Managing Director

Elegantly dignified is this impeccable small hotel in Old Town Alexandria. Rich mahogany, luxurious fabrics, sparkling crystal, and period furnishings enhance the sense of discreet opulence. Epicurean French cuisine is served in Le Chardon d'Or and more casual American fare is offered in the clublike Grill. Discriminating guests appreciate the relaxed, friendly atmosphere and thoughtful service and attention.

 42 rooms, $135/$190 EP
3 suites, $230/$385 EP
Visa, MC, Amex, Diners

 all private baths

 open year-round

children accepted
no pets

 health club, bike trails, sailing, golf, pool, D.C. historic & other attractions

 breakfast, lunch, dinner
B&B available wkends
wine & liquor available

non-smoking dining area

wheelchair access (1 room)
conference facilities (30)

From Rte. 95 take U.S. 1 (N) 1 mi. to R. on Prince St. for 1 block to L. on S. Alfred St. to hotel on R.

Prospect Hill

703-967-0844
Route 3 (Hwy. 613), Box 430, Trevilians, VA 23093
Bill & Mireille Sheehan, Innkeepers

In this restored 18th-century plantation home, with its cluster of outbuildings, guest rooms boast working fireplaces, and breakfast in bed is an option. After the blessing, guests are served a country French dinner prepared by the Sheehan family. Later, sitting beside a crackling fire or strolling about the grounds with a glass of wine, contented guests enjoy the relaxed, cordial atmosphere.

 9 rooms, $170/$190 MAP
3 suites, $190/$220 MAP
Visa, MC

all private baths, 6 Jacuzzis

closed Dec. 24 & 25

children accepted in some rooms
no pets

swimming pool, walking paths, biking, golf, horseback riding, antiquing, peace & quiet

 breakfast & dinner
wine & beer available

non-smoking dining area

conference facilities (48)

Rte. 29 (S) to Rte. 15 (S) to Zion Crossroads & Rte. 250 (E) 1 mi. to L. on Hwy. 613 for 3 mi. to inn. (Inn is 15 mi. (E) of Charlottesville via Rte. 250; 98 mi. (SW) of D.C.)

Red Fox Inn and Mosby's Tavern

703-687-6301 or 800-223-1728
2 E. Washington St., P.O. Box 385, Middleburg, VA 22117
The Reuter Family, Innkeepers

In one of the oldest incorporated towns in America, Joseph Chinn built his tavern in 1728 and called it Chinn's Ordinary. It has continued, through many changes and reincarnations, to be a popular destination for Washingtonians. Deep in hunt country, this historic inn preserves the feeling of the past along with all the modern amenities and outstanding cuisine.

 13 rooms, $115/$200 B&B
10 suites, $145/$200 B&B
Visa, MC, Amex

all private baths

open year-round

children accepted
no pets

Manassas Battlefield, Upperville Horse Show, Nat'l. Beagle Trials, polo, steeplechasing

 breakfast, lunch, dinner
wine & liquor available

smoking allowed

wheelchair access (4 rooms)
conference facilities (250)

From Washington, D.C. & Rte. 66 (W) to Rte. 50 (W) exit for 25 mi. to Middleburg & inn on R.

Trillium House

804-325-9126
Wintergreen Dr., P.O. Box 280, Wintergreen, VA 22958
Ed & Betty Dinwiddie, Innkeepers

One of the newer country inns, this was designed and built in 1983 to meet today's standards while retaining the charm of yesteryear. In the heart of Wintergreen, a year-round mountain resort, a grand assortment of activities and recreation await outside the door. Mountain country, with trees and birds and a golf course, is part of the view from the breakfast table.

 10 rooms, $80/$90 MAP
2 suites, $120/$140 MAP
Visa, MC

all private baths

closed Dec. 24 & 25

children not encouraged
no pets

skiing, golf, tennis, swimming, hiking trails, fishing, horseback riding, canoeing, antiquing

 breakfast; single entrée
fixed-price dinner Fri. & Sat.
reservation required

smoking allowed

wheelchair access (8 rooms)
conference facilities (40)

From (N) (E): I-64 (W) Exit 20 to Rte. 250 (W) to L. on Rte. 6 to Rte. 151 (S) for 14 mi. to R. on Rte. 664 for 4.5 mi. to entry. From (S): Rte. 29 (N) to L. (N) of Amherst on Rte. 151 for 21 mi. to L. on Rte. 664 as above.

WASHINGTON

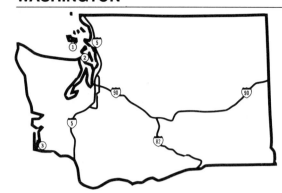

Captain Whidbey Inn, Coupeville 2
Orcas Hotel, Orcas 1
Shelburne Inn, Seaview 3

The Captain Whidbey Inn

This romantic and rustic hideaway built in 1907 on the shore of Penn Cove has the feeling of an old-fashioned New England inn. In a wonderful natural setting, where a bald eagle or a great blue heron might be glimpsed, the original inn has a big stone fireplace and quaint guest rooms, with other more modern rooms and cottages.

25 rooms, $55/$95 B&B
8 suites, $55/$95 B&B
Visa, MC, Amex, Discov

private & shared baths

open year-round

children welcome in some rooms
pets in cottages only

beach, library, boats, bikes, horseshoes, walking trails, historic towns

breakfast & lunch, peak seasons
dinner daily
wine & liquor available

non-smoking areas

conference facilities (44)

From north: I-5 (S) Exit 230 & Hwy. 20 to Coupeville. Turn on Madrona. From (S): I-5 (N) Exit 189, Mukilteo Ferry, Hwy. 525, Hwy. 20. From west: Keystone Ferry, Hwy. 20

206-678-4097
2072 W. Captain Whidbey Inn Rd., Coupeville, WA 98239
Capt. John Colby Stone, Innkeeper

Orcas Hotel

Overlooking the sea and a ferry landing, this small, beautifully restored Victorian country inn has a very authentic Northwest feeling. Its fresh Northwest cuisine, local seafood, and wine and spirits appeal to both traditionalists and young moderns alike. With warmth, color, fresh flowers, and antiques—it's like coming home to grandmother's house.

12 rooms, $48/$75 B&B
Visa, MC, Amex

private & shared baths

open year-round

preferably no children
no pets

parlor games, Moran State Park, kayaking, sailing, fishing, moped & bike rentals

breakfast, lunch, dinner
wine, beer & liquor available

non-smoking dining area

conference facilities (35)

I-5 to Hwy. 20 (W) at Burlington. Continue thru Anacortes 4 mi. (W) to ferry landing. Take ferry to Orcas. Hotel is up ramp to L.

206-376-4300
At the Ferry Landing, P.O. Box 155, Orcas, WA 98280
Barbara Jamieson, Innkeeper

Shelburne Inn

An unspoiled 28-mile stretch of wild Pacific seacoast is the setting for this inviting country inn, which has existed on this peninsula since the turn of the century. Restoration and refurbishing has included the addition of Art Nouveau stained glass windows, along with antique furnishings and fine art. Innovative cuisine has brought national recognition to the outstanding restaurant.

14 rooms, $69/$100 B&B
2 suites, $135 B&B
Visa, MC, Amex

13 private, 1 shared baths

open year-round

quiet, well-supervised children
no pets

beachcombing, bicycling, golf, horseback riding

breakfast, lunch, dinner
wine & liquor available

smoking restricted

wheelchair access (1 room)
conference facilities (35)

From Seattle, I-5 (S) to Olympia Hwy. 8 & 12 to Monsanto & Hwy. 101 (S) to Seaview. From OR coast, U.S. 101 across Astoria Bridge L. to Ilwaco (N) 2 mi. to Seaview.

206-642-2442
Pacific Hwy. 103 & 45th St., P.O. Box 250
Seaview, WA 98644
David Campiche & Laurie Anderson, Innkeepers

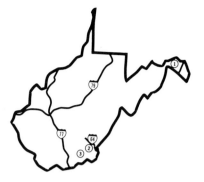

Country Inn, Berkeley Springs 1
General Lewis Inn, Lewisburg 2
Pence Springs Hotel, Pence Springs 3

The Country Inn

The homelike atmosphere of this resort-inn, with its porches, lawns, spacious lobby, and bright, comfortable guest rooms, puts guests at their ease. Further relaxation may be found in the mineral baths, massages, and European facials offered in the Renaissance Spa. Fine dining and weekend entertainment are among the many incentives for spending a refreshing vacation at this pleasant inn.

 69 rooms, $35/$75 EP
2 suites, $70/$75 EP
Visa, MC, Amex, Diners

 58 private, 3 shared baths

 open year-round

 children accepted
no pets

 health spa, golf, tennis,
fishing, boating, horseback riding

 breakfast, lunch, dinner
wine & liquor available

smoking & non-smoking rooms

 wheelchair access (36 rooms)
conference facilities (50)

I-70, Hancock, MD to Rte. 522 (S)
6 mi. to Berkeley Springs & inn on
R. From Winchester, VA, Rte. 522
(N). Inn on L.

304-258-2210 or 800-822-6630
207 So. Washington St., Berkeley Springs, WV 25411
Jack & Adele Barker, Innkeepers
Alice Clark, General Manager

The General Lewis

With over 50 other antebellum buildings in the historic district of Lewisburg listed on the National Register, the General Lewis boasts a long and eventful history. Built in 1798, it has undergone some additions and changes, but remains very true to its origins and is literally filled with treasures from the past, collected by the innkeeping family over the last 55 years.

 24 rooms, $45/$75 EP
2 suites, $70/$80 EP
Visa, MC, Amex

 all private baths

 open year-round

 children welcome
pets allowed

 garden, historic sites, golf,
swimming, hiking

 breakfast, lunch, dinner
wine & liquor available

no pipes or cigars

 conference facilities (50)

I-64, Lewisburg Exit 169 & Rte. 219
(S) for 1.5 mi. to Rte. 60 (E) for .3
mi. to inn on R.

304-645-2600
301 E. Washington St., Lewisburg, WV 24901
Mary Hock Morgan, Proprietor; Rodney Fisher, Innkeeper

Pence Springs Hotel

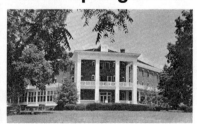

First opened in 1918, this was one of the famous old mineral spas of the Virginias. A brick plantation-style building with stately columns, overlooking the Greenbrier River Valley, it has been completely restored and refurbished and now offers sun-porch dining, a music room, and fireside lounge. Vegetable gardens supply the hotel's country-style meals and the gourmet fare of the nearby Riverside Inn.

 13 rooms, $55/$65 B&B
2 suites, $75/$125 B&B
Visa, MC, Amex, Diners, CB

 all private baths

 open year-round

 children accepted
facilities for pets in basement

 Riverside Inn gourmet dining,
croquet, bicycles, hiking, fishing,
antiquing, historic attractions

 breakfast, lunch, dinner
wine & liquor available

non-smoking dining area

wheelchair access (2 rooms)
conference facilities (200)

North/South: I-77, Beckley, I-64 (E)
to Alta Exit 161 & L. to Rte. 12S to
Alderson 11 mi. to Rte. 12S/3W for
8 mi. to Pence Springs. East/West:
I-64 to Alta Exit 161 as above.

304-445-2606
Route 3/12, Box 90, Pence Springs, WV 24962
O. Ashby Berkley, Innkeeper

WISCONSIN

Old Rittenhouse Inn, Bayfield   3
White Gull Inn, Fish Creek   1
White Lace Inn, Sturgeon Bay   2

Old Rittenhouse Inn

Three turn-of-the-century homes make up this Victorian inn where hospitality, superior dining, and music blend into a joyous whole. Mary and Jerry Phillips share in the creation of wonderful meals as well as lovely music, with dinner concerts and other enjoyable events. Guest rooms are handsomely outfitted with antiques and working fireplaces, and the entire inn offers a delightful sojourn.

 17 rooms, $69/$99 B&B
4 suites, $99/$119 B&B
Visa, MC

 all private baths

 closed winter weekdays except with advance reservations

 children accepted
pets accepted

 sailing, biking, skiing, tennis, swimming (indoor year-round)

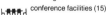 breakfast, houseguests dinner & Sun. brunch, public wine available

no smoking in dining rooms

wheelchair access (1 room)
conference facilities (15)

Duluth Hwy. 2 (E) for 60 mi. to L. on Hwy. 13 (N) (just outside Ashland) for 20 mi. to Bayfield.

715-779-5765
301 Rittenhouse Ave., P.O. Box 584, Bayfield, WI 54818
Jerry & Mary Phillips, Innkeepers

The White Gull Inn

This "New England picture perfect" landmark 1896 white clapboard inn is tucked away at the quiet end of the peninsula. Guests love the country-Victorian antiques and fireplaces that create a warm, comfortably hospitable atmosphere. Known for its food, the inn is particularly famous for the unique, traditional Door County fish boils, cooked outside over an open fire.

 14 rooms, $52/$96 EP
4 cottages, $115 EP
Visa, MC, Amex

 private & shared baths

 closed Thanksgiving Day: Dec. 24 & 25

 children welcome in suitable rooms; no pets

golf, tennis, swimming, sailing, hiking, biking, xc skiing

 breakfast, lunch, dinner beer available

smoking restricted

conference facilities (15)

Milwaukee I-43 for 79 mi. to Manitowoc & R. on Rte. 42 (N) for 85 mi. to Fish Creek. L. at stop sign for 3 blocks to inn.

414-868-3517
4225 Main St., P.O. Box 159, Fish Creek, WI 54212
Andy & Jan Coulson, Joan Holliday, &
Nancy Vaughn, Innkeepers

White Lace Inn

A winding garden pathway links the 3 beautifully restored turn-of-the-century homes comprising this charming inn. In a quiet older residential neighborhood, the inn offers guest rooms decorated with antiques, and choices among rooms with woodburning fireplaces, canopied beds, and whirlpool tubs. In the resort area of Door County, near Sturgeon Bay, there are always many vacation delights nearby.

 14 rooms, $60/$110 B&B
1 suite, $130 B&B
Visa, MC

 all private baths, 7 whirlpools

 open year-round

children over 9
no pets

 gardens, beaches, sailing, shopping, xc skiing, hiking, golf

 breakfast & snacks

6 no-smoking guest rooms

 wheelchair access (1 room)

Hwy. 57 (N) to Sturgeon Bay & Bus. Rte. 42-57 into town. Cross downtown bridge to L. on 5th Ave.

414-743-1105
16 No. 5th Ave., Sturgeon Bay, WI 54235
Dennis & Bonnie Statz, Innkeepers

Oak Bay Beach Hotel, Victoria 1
Sooke Harbour House, Sooke 2

Oak Bay Beach Hotel

This prestigious family-owned hotel in the residential area of Oak Bay is a significant part of the history and heritage of the city of Victoria. Magnificent lawns and gardens rolling to the ocean and islands and mountains in the distance provide wonderful views. The Tudor-style architecture is complemented by antiques and period pieces. Meals, service and hospitality are the best.

 45 rooms, $65/$200 EP
5 suites, $235/$375 EP
Visa, MC, Amex

 all private baths

 open year-round

 children welcome
no pets

yacht excursions, fishing, health club, golf, tennis, pool, jogging track, luncheon/dinner cruises

 breakfast, lunch, dinner
high tea, seasonal BBQ
wine & liquor available

 smoking allowed

conference facilities (140)

Follow Patricia Bay Hwy. to Hillside (E), which becomes Lansdowne. Continue to R. on Beach Dr. to hotel.

604-598-4556
1175 Beach Dr., Victoria, B.C. Canada V8S 2N2
Bruce R. Walker, Innkeeper

Sooke Harbour House Inn

Cozy and homelike, consistently rated one of Canada's top ten restaurants, this charming inn by the sea offers such luxuries as a bathtub for two with a fireplace, aesthetically designed guest rooms with gardens and porches, and a sophisticated cuisine using freshest produce from their organic vegetable & herb gardens. There are fabulous views of ocean and mountains.

 13 rooms, $80/$170 B&BL*
*includes lunch
Visa, MC

 all private baths, 7 Jacuzzis

 open year-round

 children welcome
well-behaved pets accepted

botanical & garden tours, windsurfing, scuba diving, salmon & steelhead trout fishing, hiking

 breakfast & lunch, houseguests
dinner for public
wine & liquor available

non-smoking areas

 wheelchair access (4 rooms)
conference facilities (50)

Victoria, B.C., Hwy. 1 (W) to Hwy. 14 & Sooke Village. Beyond stop lights, 1 mi. to L. on Whiffen Spit Rd. for .5 mi. to inn.

604-642-3421
1528 Whiffen Spit Rd., R.R. #4
Sooke, B.C., Canada V0S 1N0
Fredrica & Sinclair Philip, Innkeepers

Rates are quoted for 2 people for 1 night and do not necessarily include service charges and state taxes. For more detailed information, ask the inns for their brochures.

AP — American Plan (3 meals included in room rate)

MAP — Modified American Plan (breakfast & dinner included in room rate)

EP — European Plan (meals not included in room rate)

B&B — Bed & Breakfast (breakfast included in room rate)

R — represents recreational facilities and diversions either on the premises of an inn or nearby

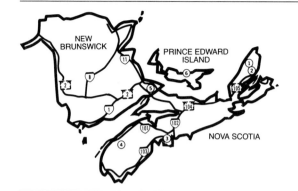

NEW BRUNSWICK

PRINCE EDWARD ISLAND

NOVA SCOTIA

Halliburton House Inn, Halifax 3
Inverary Inn, Baddeck 2
Marshlands Inn, Sackville 5
Milford House, South Milford 4
Normaway Inn, Margaree Valley 1
Shaw's Hotel, Brackley Beach 6

The Halliburton House Inn

An oasis of calm in the center of a historic city and beautiful seacoast province, this inn is an award-winning renovation of 3 c. 1809 heritage buildings. With a private garden courtyard, antique-furnished, individually decorated guest rooms, and fine evening dining by reservation, it offers an ideal home base for day trips in scenic Nova Scotia.

 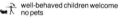 32 rooms, $75/$95 B&B
3 suites, $110/$135 B&B
Visa, MC, Amex, EnRoute

 mostly private baths

open year-round

well-behaved children welcome
no pets

 library, courtyard garden, historic touring, shopping, museums, golf

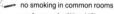 complimentary breakfast & tea
dinner by reservation
wine & liquor available

no smoking in common rooms

conference facilities (15)

In historic waterfront district of downtown Halifax, south end. On Morris St., 1 block (E) of Barrington St.

902-420-0658
5184 Morris St., Halifax, N.S. Canada B3J IB3
William McKeever, Innkeeper

Inverary Inn Resort

In the beautiful highlands of Cape Breton, this inn has recently expanded to a year-round resort, with a winter activities program, including an indoor swimming pool and health club, which is enjoyed by many. In the summer, Lake Bras d'Or offers boating and sailing and provides the fresh fish and seafood served in the waterside restaurant.

   107 rooms, $78/$90 EP
7 suites, $120/$150 EP
Visa, MC, Amex

 110 private, 4 shared baths

open year-round

children accepted
pets by permission

3 tennis courts, indoor/outdoor pool, hot tub, sauna, paddle boats, boat tours, Cabot Trail

  breakfast, lunch, dinner
wine & liquor available

no smoking in main house

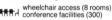 wheelchair access (8 rooms)
conference facilities (300)

From mainland Nova Scotia, follow Trans Canada Hwy. to Canso Causeway to Baddeck.

902-295-2674/In the Maritimes: 800-565-7105
P.O. Box 190, Baddeck, Victoria Country,
Nova Scotia, Canada BOE 1BO
Isobel MacAulay, Innkeeper

Marshlands Inn

Late-night hot cocoa and gingersnaps, fresh breakfast rolls and homemade bread, fresh Atlantic salmon or real steak & kidney pie for dinner are part of the at-home feeling in this graciously decorated inn. In high-ceilinged rooms, guests relax by the fire or read in the library. Walking in the flower and vegetable gardens is another pleasure here.

   24 rooms, $49/$65 EP
1 suite, $70/$85 B&B
Visa, MC, Amex, EnRoute

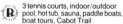 15 private, 5 shared baths

closed Dec. & Jan.

children welcome
small pets allowed

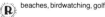 beaches, birdwatching, golf

  breakfast, luncheon, dinner
wine & liquor available

smoking allowed

 wheelchair access (5 rooms)
conference facilities (35)

From Monckton, Hwy. 2 (S) to Exit 541 for .7 mi. to traffic light 200 yds. on R.

506-536-0170
73 Bridge St., Box 1440
Sackville, N. B. Canada EOA 3CO
John & Mary Blakely, Innkeepers

Milford House

A blue heron flashes by, a loon's haunting cry echoes across the placid lake, and far across the water two people are paddling a canoe. This scene might be experienced from one of the tidy, rustic cabins that intermittently wreathe the shores of two lakes in this unspoiled wilderness area. Or there's the main lodge of this historic hotel, with a library and hearty, wholesome meals.

 65 rooms, $115/$125 MAP (rooms are in 26 cabins) no credit cards

 all cabins with private baths

 closed Sept. 15 to June 15

 children welcome
pets welcome

 canoeing, swimming, tennis, croquet, hiking, nat'l. park, craft shops, museums

 breakfast, dinner
packed lunches

 smoking allowed

wheelchair access (1 cabin)
conference facilities (30)

Yarmouth, Hwy. 101 to Annapolis Royal & R. on Hwy. 8 for 10 mi. to inn. From Halifax: Hwy. 101 to Annapolis Royal & Hwy. 8 for 15 mi. to inn.

902-532-2617
South Milford, R.R. #4
Annapolis Royal, N. S. Canada BOS IAO
Warren & Margaret Miller, Innkeepers

Normaway Inn

On 250 acres in the hills of the famed Margaree River Valley, near the beginning of Cape Breton's spectacular Cabot Trail, this homey, informal inn offers rooms in the lodge, cabins—most with woodstove fireplaces—superb food, service, and choice wines. Guests often relax by the fire after dinner and enjoy films or traditional entertainment.

 26 rooms, $70/$90 (Canadian) EP $125/$135 (Canadian) MAP Visa, MC, Amex

 all private baths

 closed Oct. 16 to June 14

 children accepted
pets by prior arrangement

tennis, hiking, biking, lawn games, recreation barn, canoeing, salmon fishing, cruises, beaches

 breakfast & dinner
packed lunches
wine & liquor available

no smoking in dining room

 wheelchair access (2 rooms)
conference facilities (50)

Trans Canada Hwy. Jct. 7 at Nyanza (N) on Cabot Trail 17 mi. Between Lake O'Law and N.E. Margaree turn at Egypt Rd. 2 mi. to inn.

800-565-9463 or 902-248-2987
(off-season: 902-564-5433)
P.O. Box 138, Margaree Valley, N. S. Canada BOE 2CO
David M. MacDonald, Innkeeper

Shaw's Hotel

The Shaw family turned their original 1793 pioneer farm into an inn in 1860. It served a real need in this popular resort area, with its wild seascapes, breathtaking views, and one of Canada's finest national parks. Robbie Shaw says there is much to do here for both children and adults, and meals are good and plentiful for hearty appetites.

 27 rooms, $79/$144 (Canadian) MAP 18 cotts., $115/$200 (Canadian) MAP Visa, Amex

 private & shared baths, 2 Jacuzzis

 closed Oct. 1 to June 1

 children accepted
pets in cottages only

 sailing, canoeing, walking paths, golf, ocean swimming, tennis

 breakfast, dinner
wine & liquor available

smoking allowed

conference facilities (30)

Take ferry or plane to P.E.I. Trans Canada Hwy. (Rte. 1) to Charlottetown. Follow signs to airport and Rte. 15 for 10 mi. to Brackley Beach.

902-672-2022
Brackley Beach, Prince Edward Island
Canada COA 2HO
Robbie Shaw, Innkeeper

Rates are quoted for 2 people for 1 night and do not necessarily include service charges and state taxes. For more detailed information, ask the inns for their brochures.

AP — American Plan (3 meals included in room rate)

MAP — Modified American Plan (breakfast & dinner included in room rate)

EP — European Plan (meals not included in room rate)

B&B — Bed & Breakfast (breakfast included in room rate)

 — represents recreational facilities and diversions either on the premises of an inn or nearby

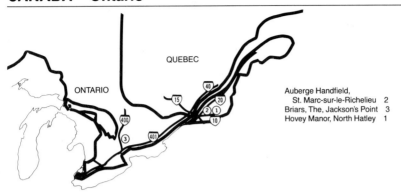

QUEBEC

ONTARIO

Auberge Handfield,
St. Marc-sur-le-Richelieu 2
Briars, The, Jackson's Point 3
Hovey Manor, North Hatley 1

Auberge Handfield

Quintessentially French is this inn on the Richelieu River in an ancient French-Canadian village, where French is universally spoken. The somewhat rustic decor of this venerable 150-year-old mansion is complemented with antiques and locally crafted furnishings. A marina and other resort facilities, along with the outstanding French cuisine make this a fascinating and enjoyable holiday experience.

 55 rooms, $50/$105 EP
7 suites, $130/$185 EP
Visa, MC, Amex, EnRoute

 all private baths, 11 Jacuzzis

 open year-round

 children accepted
no pets; kennel nearby

 swimming pool, ping-pong, skating, theater, sugar shack, bicycle ride, boating, golf, tennis

breakfast, lunch, dinner
wine & liquor available

smoking allowed

wheelchair access (20 rooms)
conference facilities (130)

From Hwy. 20 Exit 112 (Beloeil/St. Marc) turn L. on Rte. 223 (N) for about 10 km to inn.

514-584-2226
555 Chemin du Prince, St. Marc-sur-Richelieu
Quebec, Canada JOL 2EO
M. & Mme. Conrad Handfield, Innkeepers

The Briars

The Sibbald family has owned this 200-acre estate since 1840, and in 1922 founded the Briars Golf & Country Club. Gradually the estate became the lively, 5-star resort-inn it is today. Sibbald family art and heirlooms adorn public areas. Guests enjoy the fresh, homemade, sophisticated meals and the charm and fun of this special place with its lawns, gardens, woods, and lake.

 80 rooms, $180/$206 (Canadian) AP
11 suites, $238/$266 (Canadian) AP
Visa, MC

 all private baths

 open year-round

 children accepted
no pets; kennels nearby

 swimming, whirlpool & sauna, golf, tennis, xc skiing, fishing, sailing, ice-fishing, windsurfing

breakfast, lunch, dinner
wine & liquor available

no pipes/cigars in dining room

wheelchair access (14 rooms)
conference facilities (75)

Toronto Hwy. 404 (N) to R. (E) on Aurora Rd. to L. (N) on Woodbine Ave. 20 mi. to Sutton. L. (N) on Dalton Rd. to Jackson's Pt. R. (E) on Lakeshore Rd. .6 mi. to Hedge Rd. & inn.

416-722-3271
Hedge Rd., Box 100
Jackson's Point, Ontario, Canada LOE ILO
John & Barbara Sibbald, Innkeepers

Hovey Manor

Formerly a private estate modeled on Mt. Vernon, this gracious manor abounds with antiques and flowers in a romantic lakeside setting. The guest rooms are individually decorated and many feature woodburning fireplaces, private balconies, and whirlpool tubs. The inn's acclaimed cuisine and a full range of year-round recreational facilities right on site make Hovey Manor a destination in itself.

 35 rooms, $120/$275
(Canadian) MAP
Visa, MC, Amex, Diners

 all private baths, 7 Jacuzzis

 open year-round

 children accepted
no pets

 all water sports, tennis, 35 km xc ski trails, alpine skiing, golf, riding

breakfast, lunch, dinner
wine & liquor available

non-smoking dining area

wheelchair access (2 rooms)
conference facilities (75)

VT. I-91 (N) to border; Rte. 55N for 29 kms. to No. Hatley Exit 29 & Rte. 108 (E) for 9 kms. to No. Hatley & Hovey Manor signs.

819-842-2421
Hovey Rd. (P.O. Box 60)
No. Hatley, Quebec, Canada JOB 2CO
Steve & Kathryn Stafford, Innkeepers

INDEX